Contents

Quarktaler

Nutritional values: kcal: 76 Carbohydrates: 6 g Protein: 2 g Fat: 2 g

Ingredients:

- 3 eggs
- 250 g low-fat quark
- 100 g of oat bran
- 50 g wheat bran
- 25 g of flaxseed
- 1 sachet of baking powder
- 1 teaspoon salt
- Lemon juice

Preparation:

1. Preheat the oven to 190 degrees and set it to circulating air.
2. Put all the ingredients in a bowl and mix them well.
3. Shape the whole thing into 12 equal portions.
4. Place the portions on a baking sheet that you previously lined with baking paper and flatten them a little.
5. Bake the thalers for 25 minutes.
6. Let them cool down and enjoy them.

Low-carb bread with sunflower seeds

Nutritional values: kcal: 1100

Ingredients:

- 2 eggs
- 250 g low-fat quark
- 50 g sunflower seeds
- 50 g of crushed flaxseed
- 50 g wheat bran
- 50 g protein powder
- 1 teaspoon Baking powder
- 1 teaspoon salt

Preparation:

1. Preheat the oven to 200 degrees.
2. Mix together all of the dry ingredients.
3. Add the quark and eggs and knead them into a dough.
4. Let everything steep for 10 minutes.
5. Shape a loaf of bread and place it on a parchment-lined baking sheet.
6. Bake for 40 minutes.

Pancakes with berries

Nutritional values: kcal: 298 Carbohydrates: 26 g Protein: 21 g Fat: 9 g

Ingredients:

Pancake:

- 1 egg
- 50 g spelled flour

- 50 g almond flour
- 15 g coconut flour

Filling:

- 40 g mixed berries
- 10 g chocolate

- 150 ml of water
- salt

- 5 g powdered sugar
- 4 tbsp yogurt

Preparation:

1. Put the flour, egg, and some salt in a blender jar.
2. Add 150 ml of water.
3. Mix everything with a whisk.
4. Mix everything into a batter.
5. Heat a coated pan.
6. Put in half of the batter.
7. Once the pancake is firm, turn it over.
8. Take out the pancake and add the second half of the batter to the pan and repeat.
9. Meanwhile, melt the chocolate over a water bath.
10. Let the pancakes cool.
11. Brush the pancakes with the yogurt.
12. Wash the berry and let it drain.
13. Put the berries on top of the yogurt.
14. Roll up the pancakes.
15. Sprinkle them with the powdered sugar.
16. Decorate the whole thing with the melted chocolate.

Omelette à la Margherita

Nutritional values: kcal: 402 Carbohydrates: 7 g Protein: 1 g Fat: 4 g

Ingredients:

- 3 eggs
- 50 g parmesan cheese
- 2 tbsp heavy cream
- 1 tbsp olive oil

For covering:

- 3 - 4 stalks of basil
- 1 tomato

- 1 teaspoon oregano
- nutmeg
- salt
- pepper

- 100 g grated mozzarella

Preparation:

1. Mix the eggs and cream in a bowl.
2. Add the grated parmesan, nutmeg, oregano, pepper and salt and stir everything.
3. Heat the oil in a pan.

4. Add half of the egg mixture to the pan.

5. Let the omelette set over medium heat, turn it, and then remove it.

6. Repeat with the second half of the egg mixture.

7. Cut the tomatoes into slices and place them on top of the omelets.

8. Scatter the mozzarella over the tomatoes.

9. Place the omelets on a baking sheet.

10. Cook them in an oven at 180 degrees for 5 to 10 minutes.

11. Then take the omelets out and decorate them with the basil leaves.

Omelette with tomatoes and green onions

Nutritional values: kcal: 263 Carbohydrates: 8 g Protein: 3 g Fat: 4 g

Ingredients:

- 6 eggs
- 2 tomatoes
- 2 spring onions
- 1 shallot
- 2 tbsp butter
- 1 tbsp olive oil
- 1 pinch of nutmeg
- salt
- pepper

Preparation:

1. Whisk the eggs in a bowl.

2. Mix them together and season them with salt and pepper.

3. Peel the shallot and chop it up.

4. Clean the onions and cut them into rings.

5. Wash the tomatoes and cut them into pieces.

6. Heat the oil and butter in a pan.

7. Braise half of the shallots in it.

8. Add half the egg mixture.

9. Let everything set over medium heat.

10. Scatter a few tomatoes and onion rings on top.

11. Repeat with the second half of the egg mixture.

12. At the end, spread the grated nutmeg over the whole thing.

Coconut chia pudding with berries

Nutritional values: kcal: 662 Carbohydrates: 8 g Protein: 8 g Fat: 5 g

Ingredients:

- 150 g raspberries and blueberries
- 60 g chia seeds
- 500 ml coconut milk
- 1 teaspoon agave syrup
- ½ teaspoon ground bourbon vanilla

Preparation:

1. Put the chia seeds, agave syrup, and vanilla in a bowl.
2. Pour in the coconut milk.
3. Mix everything well and let it soak for 30 minutes.
4. Meanwhile, wash the berries and let them drain well.
5. Divide the coconut chia pudding between two glasses.
6. Put the berries on top.

Smoked salmon with salad

Nutritional values: kcal: 195 Carbohydrates: 1 g Protein: 22 g Fat: 8 g

Ingredients:

- 100 g smoked salmon
- 50 g lettuce
- 4 cherry tomatoes
- ½ organic lemon
- 2 stalks of dill

Preparation:

1. Wash the lettuce leaves, shake them dry, and chop them up.
2. Wash the tomatoes and cut them in half.
3. Wash the dill and shake it dry.
4. Cut the lemon into thin slices.
5. Arrange the lettuce, tomatoes, and salmon on a plate.
6. Drizzle some lemon juice over it, add the dill and serve everything.

Red cabbage, radishes, and spring onion salad

Nutritional values: kcal: 2 Carbohydrates: 1 g Protein: 2 g Fat: 4 g

Ingredients:

- 8 radishes
- 3 spring onions
- ½ small red cabbage
- ½ bunch of parsley
- Juice of half a lemon
- 1 tbsp olive oil
- 2 teaspoons agave syrup
- salt
- pepper

Preparation:

1. Brush and wash the red cabbage.
2. Cut into fine strips with a knife.
3. Mix it with salt and knead everything thoroughly.

4. Let everything steep for 30 minutes.

5. Wash the onions and cut only the green inside into fine rings.

6. Clean, rinse, and cut the radishes in half. Then cut them into slices.

7. Mix the red cabbage with lemon juice, agave syrup, and olive oil.

8. Fold in the onion and radishes.

9. Season everything with the parsley and pepper.

Salad with pear, rocket, feta and walnuts

Nutritional values: kcal: 593 Carbohydrates: 26 g Protein: 14 g Fat: 46 g

Ingredients:

- 140 g pear
- 50 g rocket
- 50 g feta
- 30 g walnuts
- 30 g pomegranate seeds
- 2 tbsp avocado oil
- salt
- pepper

Preparation:

1. Wash the arugula and drain it.

2. Remove the too long stems.

3. Arrange the salad on a plate.

4. Wash the pear and let it dry off.

5. Quarter the pear and cut out the core. Then cut them into slices.

6. Cut the feta into cubes.

7. Spread the feta and pear on the lettuce leaves.

8. Season everything with salt and pepper and drizzle the oil over it.

9. Sprinkle everything with roughly chopped walnuts and serve.

Mixed salad with oranges and walnuts

Nutritional values: kcal: 295 Carbohydrates: 4 g Protein: 2 g Fat: 26 g

Ingredients:

- 1 orange
- 250 g mixed lettuce
- 100 g peeled walnut kernels

For the dressing:

- 4 tbsp olive oil
- 2 tbsp orange juice
- 1 teaspoon lemon juice
- ½ teaspoon agave syrup
- ½ teaspoon mustard
- salt
- pepper

Preparation:

1. Clean and drain the lettuce.

2. Peel the orange and peel off the white skin.

3. Cut out the fruit fillets from the orange.

4. Toast the walnuts in a pan without oil and set them aside.

5. Mix 2 tablespoons of orange juice with mustard, agave syrup, salt and pepper. Then stir in the olive oil.

6. Put the salad in a bowl.

7. Add the orange pieces and mix everything together.

8. Arrange the whole thing on 4 plates with the walnuts and the dressing.

Tomato salad with cucumber and apple

Nutritional values: kcal: 105 Carbohydrates: 23 g Protein: 2 g Fat: 1 g

Ingredients:

- ½ red onion
- 300 g small tomatoes
- 300 g cucumber
- 200 g apple
- Chopped parsley
- Juice of half a lemon
- salt
- pepper

Preparation:

1. Wash and dry the tomatoes, cucumber, and apple. Cut everything into small pieces.

2. Peel the onion and cut it into cubes.

3. Mix the tomatoes, cucumber, apple, onion, and parsley with lemon juice.

4. Season the whole thing with salt and pepper and serve.

Pumpkin soup with roasted cashew nuts

Nutritional values: kcal: 345 Carbohydrates: 20 g Protein: 1 g Fat: 27 g

Ingredients:

- 2 carrots
- 1 shallot
- ½ Hokkaido pumpkin
- ½ chilli pepper
- 40 g butter
- 750 ml vegetable stock
- 100 ml orange juice
- ginger
- 1 tbsp lemon juice
- 4 tbsp pumpkin seed oil
- 4 tbsp cashew nuts
- 4 flowers of nasturtium
- Chopped parsley
- salt
- pepper

Preparation:

1. Wash and dry the pumpkin.

2. Cut it in half and remove the seeds.

3. Cut one of the halves into small pieces.

4. Peel the carrots and cut them into slices.

5. Peel the shallot and dice it.

6. Peel the ginger and chop it into small pieces.

7. Halve the chili pepper, core it and cut it into pieces.

8. Melt butter in a saucepan and sweat the shallot in it.

9. Add the carrots and pumpkin and sauté everything.

10. Deglaze the whole thing with the stock and pour it on.

11. Add the chili pepper and let everything cook, covered, for 15 minutes.

12. Roast the cashew nuts in a pan without fat.

13. Take out the cashew nuts and chop them.

14. Stir the ginger, lemon juice, and orange juice into the soup.

15. Take the pan off the stove and puree everything with a hand blender.

16. Season everything with salt and pepper and put it in bowls.

17. Drizzle everything with the pumpkin seed oil and sprinkle the parsley and cashew nuts on top.

Cream of pea soup

Nutritional values: kcal: 577 Carbohydrates: 20 g Protein: 15 g Fat: 42 g

Ingredients

- 1 lemon
- 1 onion
- 1 clove of garlic
- 400 g peas
- 100 g leek
- 500 ml vegetable stock
- 200 ml of cream
- 2 tbsp olive oil
- Grated ginger
- salt
- pepper

Preparation:

1. Peel the onions and garlic and cut them into cubes.

2. Wash the leek and cut it into rings.

3. Wash the lemon and cut in half.

4. Rub one half and squeeze out the other half.

5. Heat the olive oil in a saucepan and sauté the onion, garlic and leek.

6. Add the peas and pour the stock on top.

7. Add salt and pepper.

8. Cover everything and let it simmer over a medium flame for 10 minutes. Stir it from time to time.

9. Add the ginger and grated lemon to the soup.

10. Take the pan off the stove and puree the contents with a hand blender.

11. Add the cream and mix everything again.

12. Season everything with the lemon juice and salt and pepper.

Salad bowl with avocado and mozzarella

Nutritional values: kcal: 38 Carbohydrates: 1 g Protein: 9 g Fat: 33 g

Ingredients:

- 60 g avocado
- 50 g tomatoes
- 40 g mozzarella
- 30 g mixed salad
- 2 tbsp olive oil
- 1 stick of basil
- salt
- pepper

Preparation:

1. Wash the lettuce leaves and let them dry well. Then pluck them into pieces.
2. Put the pieces in a bowl.
3. Wash the tomatoes and cut them into slices.
4. Tick off the mozzarella.
5. Wash the basil and shake it dry. Then pluck the leaves off.
6. Halve the avocado and remove the stone.
7. Remove the pulp from the skin and cut it into strips.
8. Add the avocado, tomatoes, mozzarella, and basil to the salar in the bowl.
9. Drizzle everything with the olive oil and season with salt and pepper.

Beetroot salad with orange and feta

Nutritional values: kcal: 186 Carbohydrates: 22 g Protein: 1 g Fat: 2 g

Ingredients:

- 200 g beetroot
- 70 g peeled orange
- 30 g feta
- 1 stick of mint
- 1 teaspoon lime juice
- Chilli flakes
- salt
- pepper

Preparation:

1. Peel the beetroot and cut it into slices.
2. Divide the oranges into pieces, remove the skin, and cut them into slices.
3. Fan the beetroot and orange slices alternately on a plate.
4. Wash the mint and shake it dry. Pluck the leaves off.
5. Mash the feta and spread it over the beetroot and oranges.
6. Drizzle everything with lime juice and sprinkle the mint and chili flakes on top.
7. Season everything with salt and pepper.

Pumpkin soup with pumpkin seeds and ginger

Nutritional values: kcal: 178 Carbohydrates: 13 g Protein: 2 g Fat: 9 g

Ingredients:

- 2 carrots
- 1 shallot
- ½ pumpkin
- 600 - 750 ml of water
- 2 tbsp pumpkin seeds
- 1 tbsp butter
- 1 tbsp olive oil
- 4 tsp sour cream, organic
- 1 teaspoon lime juice
- 3 cm ginger
- salt
- pepper

Preparation:

1. Wash and dry the pumpkin.
2. Cut it in two.
3. Remove the seeds.
4. Cut the meat into cubes.
5. Peel the carrots and cut them into cubes.
6. Repeat for the shallot.
7. Heat butter and olive oil in a saucepan and sweat the shallot in it.
8. Add the carrots, pumpkins and sauté the whole thing, stirring constantly.
9. Deglaze the vegetables with a little water and loosen the roast by stirring.
10. Pour the whole thing up with water and let it simmer covered for 10 to 15 minutes.
11. Peel the ginger.
12. Take some liquid out of the pot and put it in a blender jar.
13. Add the ginger and puree the whole thing.
14. Add the ginger water to the soup.
15. Take the pan off the stove and puree the contents with a hand blender.
16. Season to taste with lime juice, salt and pepper.
17. Pour the soup into bowls and stir in 1 teaspoon of sour cream.
18. Sprinkle everything with the pumpkin seeds and serve.

Homemade tomato soup with meatballs

Nutritional values: kcal: 292 Carbohydrates: 10 g Protein: 31 g Fat: 11 g

Ingredients:

For the soup:

- 2 shallots
- 2 celery stalks
- 2 cloves of garlic
- 1 red chili pepper

- 400 g tomatoes
- 400 ml passata
- 1 tbsp olive oil

For the meatballs:

- 1 egg
- 4 stalks of parsley
- 2 sprigs of thyme
- 400 g ground beef
- 150 g low carb noodles
- salt
- pepper
- 1 tbsp yogurt
- 1 tbsp olive oil
- pepper
- salt

Preparation:

1. Wash the tomatoes, dry them, and cut them in half. Remove the stalk.
2. Cut the tomatoes into pieces.
3. Peel the shallots and cut them into cubes.
4. Clean the celery and cut it into slices.
5. Peel the garlic and press it.
6. Cut the chili in half, core and chop.
7. Heat the olive oil in a large saucepan and sweat the shallots with the garlic in it.
8. Add the celery and tomatoes and heat everything, stirring constantly.
9. Add the passata and chili pepper and bring to the boil.
10. Cover and let everything simmer over medium heat.
11. Wash the herbs and shake them dry.
12. Pluck the leaves and chop them up.
13. Beat the egg in a bowl and add the minced meat, yogurt, and herbs.
14. Season the whole thing with salt and pepper.
15. Form small balls out of the ground beef mixture.
16. Heat the olive oil in a pan and fry the meatballs all over.
17. Take out the meatballs and set them aside.
18. Prepare the low carb noodles according to their instructions and then let them drain in a colander.
19. Taste the tomato soup.
20. Add the meatballs and noodles and serve while it's still hot.

Express pan with steak and broccoli

Nutritional values: kcal: 350 Carbohydrates: 8 g Protein: 39 g Fat: 16 g

Ingredients:

- 2 onions
- 1 piece of ginger

- 600 g hip steak
- 500 g broccoli
- 60 g nut mix
- 4 tbsp soy sauce
- 2 tablespoons oil
- salt
- pepper
- cumin
- coriander

Preparation:

1. Clean, wash, and chop the broccoli.
2. Cook the broccoli in salted boiling water for 2 minutes. Then pour it off and put it off and let it drain.
3. Pat the meat dry and cut it into strips.
4. Peel the onions and cut them into cubes.
5. Peel the ginger and finely chop it.
6. Chop the nuts.
7. Fry the meat vigorously in hot oil for 2 to 3 minutes.
8. Season it with salt and pepper and then take it out.
9. Add the broccoli, onions, ginger and nuts along with ¼ teaspoon cumin and coriander to the frying fat and fry for 2 to 3 minutes.
10. Add the soy sauce and 4 tablespoons of water as well as the meat. Taste everything and serve it.

Warm lamb's lettuce with chicken fillet skewers

Nutritional values: kcal: 229 Carbohydrates: 15 g Protein: 17 g Fat: 10 g

Ingredients:

- 2 chicken fillets
- 1 pear
- 1 onion
- 100 g lamb's lettuce
- 100 ml orange juice
- Some radicchio
- 4 tbsp sunflower oil
- 2 tbsp sugar
- 2 tbsp balsamic vinegar
- salt
- pepper

Preparation:

1. Wash the meat and pat it dry. Cut it into cubes.
2. Put the cubes on wooden skewers.
3. Wash the lettuce and shake it dry.
4. Wash the radicchio and cut it into strips.
5. Wash the pear, cut it into quarters, and remove the core.
6. Cut the quarters into wedges.

7. Peel and cut the onions into cubes.

8. Heat 2 tablespoons of oil in a pan.

9. Fry the onion in it and caramelize the sugar.

10. Deglaze everything with vinegar and orange juice.

11. Fold in the lamb's lettuce, pear, and radicchio.

12. Heat 2 tablespoons of oil in a pan. Fry the skewers in it for 5 minutes, turning them several times.

13. Season the skewers with salt and pepper.

14. Place the meat skewers and salad on a plate and serve with the dressing.

Acropolis meatballs with bell pepper and zucchini vegetables

Nutritional values: kcal: 572 Carbohydrates: 9 g Protein: 35 g Fat: 41 g

Ingredients:

- 2 large peppers
- 1 egg
- 1 zucchini
- 6 stalks of thyme
- 500 g mixed mince
- 100 g feta
- 4 tbsp olive oil
- 3 tbsp breadcrumbs
- 1 tbsp black olives without stones
- salt
- pepper

Preparation:

1. Preheat the oven and set it to fan oven.

2. Line a baking sheet with parchment paper.

3. Knead the mince with the egg, breadcrumbs, 1 teaspoon salt and ½ pepper.

4. Shape the mixture into 4 large meatballs.

5. Heat 2 tablespoons of oil in a large pan and fry the meatballs over medium heat for 3 minutes on each side.

6. Wash the thyme and shake it dry. Peel off the leaves.

7. Crumble the feta.

8. Mix the feta with 2/3 of the thyme and olives.

9. Place the meatballs on the baking sheet and spread the mixture over them.

10. Bake everything in the oven for 8 minutes.

11. Brush and wash the zucchini and peppers.

12. Cut the zucchini lengthways into thin strips.

13. Cut the peppers into cubes.

14. Heat the rest of the oil in the frying fat of the meatballs.

15. Fry the peppers, zucchini and the remaining thyme for 4 to 5 minutes, turning occasionally.

16. Season the vegetables with salt and pepper.

17. Serve it with the meatballs.

Phad Thai with Shirataki noodles

Nutritional values: kcal: 326 Carbohydrates: 8 g Protein: 33 g Fat: 12 g

Ingredients:

- 2 carrots
- 2 cloves of garlic
- 1 egg
- 1 small, red chili pepper
- 200 g chicken fillet
- 125 g mung bean sprouts
- 80 g spring onions
- 4 tbsp soy sauce
- 2 tbsp fish sauce
- 2 tbsp tamarind sauce
- 4 teaspoons of oil
- 2 packs of shirataki noodles
- salt
- pepper
- Lime wedges

Preparation:

1. Peel the carrots and cut them into fine sticks.
2. Clean the spring onions and cut them into rings.
3. Wash the sprouts and let them drain.
4. Peel and chop the garlic.
5. Wash the chili, cut it in half lengthways and remove the seeds. Then cut it into rings.
6. Wash the chicken fillet, pat it dry and cut it into strips.
7. Heat 2 teaspoons of oil in a pan and stir-fry the meat.
8. Add half of the garlic, chili, soy sauce, fish sauce and tamarind sauce and stir everything in.
9. Take everything out of the pan.
10. Prepare the pasta according to the instructions on the packet.
11. Add 1 teaspoon of oil to the hot pan and fry the carrots, spring onions and sprouts in it for 3 to 4 minutes, stirring constantly.
12. Add the noodles, the remaining garlic, chili, soy sauce, fish sauce and tamarind sauce and fry everything for 1 to 2 minutes.
13. Whisk the egg, 2 tablespoons of water, salt and pepper.
14. Heat 1 teaspoon of oil in a small pan and add the mixture.
15. Let them set slightly and stir them into a scrambled egg.
16. Lift the scrambled eggs and chicken strips into the vegetable noodles and heat everything briefly.
17. Serve the whole thing on two plates and garnish with lime wedges.

Cream of spinach soup with Madras curry

Nutritional values: kcal: 503 Carbohydrates: 15 g Protein: 11 g Fat: 43 g

Ingredients:

- 2 onions
- 2 cloves of garlic
- 1 piece of ginger
- 1 can of unsweetened coconut milk
- 500 g baby spinach
- 3 tbsp lime juice
- 2 tbsp sunflower oil
- 1 tbsp butter
- Red Madras curry powder
- salt
- pepper
- sugar

Preparation:

1. Wash and drain the spinach.
2. Set aside a handful of the spinach.
3. Cut up the rest.
4. Peel the ginger, onions and garlic and cut everything into cubes.
5. Heat oil and butter in a saucepan and sauté the ginger, the onions and the garlic.
6. Dust 1 tbsp curry over it and sweat it all for a short time.
7. Pour in the coconut milk and 200 ml of water and let everything boil. Then season it with salt, pepper and 1 tablespoon of sugar.
8. Cover and let everything cook over medium heat for 10 minutes.
9. After 5 minutes, add the chopped spinach.
10. Puree the soup, add salt and lime juice to taste.
11. Serve the soup with the remaining spinach.

Minced meat pot with kohlrabi

ngredients:

- 2 kohlrabi
- 1 onion
- 250 g mince
- 330 ml vegetable broth
- 80 ml of cream
- 1 tbsp olive oil
- salt
- pepper

Preparation:

1. Wash and peel the kohlrabi.
2. Cut it into thin slices.
3. Peel the onions and cut them into cubes.
4. Heat olive oil in a non-stick pan.
5. Fry the onions and minced meat in it.
6. Add the kohlrabi and steam everything.
7. Deglaze the whole thing with the vegetable stock and let it cook for 15 minutes.
8. Add the cream and season with salt and pepper.

Cevapcici and vegetable gratin

Ingredients:

- 3 peppers, red, yellow and green
- 2 zucchini
- 1 kg frozen cevapcici
- 250 g Gouda
- 200 ml of cream
- 200 ml of milk
- 4 tbsp flour
- Some tomato paste
- salt
- pepper
- Paprika powder

Preparation:

1. Spread the frozen cevapcici in a baking dish and put them in the oven.
2. Bake them at 200 degrees until they turn brown.
3. Wash the peppers and zucchini and cut them into pieces.
4. Fry both in a pan with a little fat.
5. Whisk the cream with the milk and flour.
6. Add the mixture to the vegetables.
7. Add the tomato paste, season everything with salt and pepper and let it simmer for a few minutes.
8. Put the vegetables over the cevapcici.
9. Sprinkle the grated cheese on top and let it bake in the oven again until the cheese is lightly brown.

Greek zucchini casserole with feta

Ingredients:

- 2 zucchini
- 1 onion
- 1 clove of garlic
- 400 g ground beef
- 200 g feta
- 100 ml of water
- 1 tbsp tomato paste
- ½ stock cube
- olive oil
- thyme
- oregano
- basil
- salt
- pepper

Preparation:

1. Chop the onion and garlic.
2. Cut the zucchini into slices.
3. Take a mold and grease it with the olive oil.
4. Put the zucchini slices in the mold.
5. Preheat the oven to 150 degrees.

6. Fry the minced meat a little in olive oil.

7. Add the onions and garlic and cook until the onions are translucent.

8. Stir in the tomato paste.

9. Season everything to taste and rub off with water.

10. Add half the stock cube.

11. Stew everything over medium heat for 5 to 10 minutes.

12. Season it with salt and pepper.

13. Add half of the mince mixture to the zucchini.

14. Top it with the feta.

15. Layer more zucchini on top, top with the rest of the mince mixture and then top with the feta.

16. Put everything in the oven and bake for 20 to 25 minutes.

Mediterranean tuna pizza

Ingredients:

- 3 eggs
- 1 artichoke
- 1 onion
- 300 g canned tuna
- 150 g feta
- 30 g grated parmesan cheese
- 3 tablespoons water
- 2 tbsp capers
- 1 tbsp tomato paste
- 1 teaspoon herbs of Provence
- salt
- pepper

Preparation:

1. Drain the tuna well, transfer it to a bowl and mash it with a fork.

2. Add the eggs and mix everything well.

3. Line a baking sheet with baking paper and pour the mixture on top.

4. Preheat the oven to 180 degrees and add the tray.

5. Bake for 15 minutes.

6. Mix the tomato paste with the water, salt and pepper and the herbs of Provence to a sauce.

7. Cut the onion into fine rings and split the artichoke.

8. Cut the feta into thin slices.

9. Take the tuna out of the oven and spread the tomato sauce on top.

10. Top with the capers, artichokes, and onions.

11. This is followed by the feta and on top of that the parmesan.

12. Put the pizza back in the oven and bake it for 30 minutes at 180 degrees.

Tomato and basil soup

Ingredients:

- 1 shallot
- 1 clove of garlic
- 800 g ripe tomatoes
- 20 g butter
- 250 ml vegetable broth
- 4 teaspoons of olive oil
- 8 basil leaves
- salt
- pepper
- Stevia

Preparation:

1. Score a cross on the stem of the tomato and add it to boiling water. Then put them off with cold water.
2. Peel off the tomato skin and dice the peeled tomatoes.
3. Peel the shallot and garlic and finely chop them. Also chop the four basil leaves.
4. Melt the butter in a saucepan and add the shallot and garlic.
5. After sautéing briefly, add the tomato pieces to the pan and steam everything.
6. Then pour on the broth and let the soup simmer covered for 10 minutes.
7. Puree the soup and pour it through a fine sieve to remove the shallot and tomato seeds.
8. Stir in the chopped basil.
9. Season everything with salt, pepper and stevia.
10. Serve the soup on four plates and garnish with 1 teaspoon of olive oil and 1 leaf of basil each.

Cheese cakes with ground turkey

Ingredients:

- 1 egg
- 1 onion
- 400 g ground turkey
- 120 g of grated cheese
- 1 teaspoon curry paste
- salt
- pepper
- Paprika powder
- Chili powder
- garlic

Preparation:

1. Mix the mince with the grated cheese and egg.
2. Season everything with salt, pepper, chilli, paprika and the curry paste.
3. Add a chopped onion and chopped garlic.
4. Let everything go for a moment.
5. Shape several meatballs out of the mixture and press them flat.
6. Let a pan get hot and add some oil.
7. Fry the meatballs until golden brown on both sides.

Bell pepper chicken pan with mango sauce

Ingredients:

- 1 red pepper
- 1 onion
- 1 clove of garlic
- 1 mango
- 200 g chicken breast fillet
- 100 ml vegetable broth
- 2 tbsp cream cheese
- 1 teaspoon tomato paste
- chives
- salt
- pepper
- Paprika powder
- chili
- oil

Preparation:

1. Cut the onion into rings and the pepper into strips.
2. Cut the fillets into 3 parts.
3. Cut the mango into small cubes and chop the garlic.
4. Heat some oil in a small saucepan and briefly sweat the mango and garlic in it.
5. Deglaze both with the vegetable stock and let it simmer covered for 10 minutes.
6. Heat oil in a large pan and sweat the pepper in it.
7. Add the fillets and onions and cook for 5 minutes.
8. Season the whole thing with the paprika powder.
9. Take the mango sauce off the stove and stir in the tomato paste and cream cheese. Season with salt, pepper and chili.
10. Add the chives to the sauce and arrange the fillets on a plate with the peppers and pour the sauce over them.

Egg lasagne

Ingredients:

- 6 eggs
- 1 onion
- 1 cup of crème fraîche
- 1 can of tomatoes
- 500 g mince
- 200 g of grated cheese
- 100 ml cream
- 1 packet of strained tomatoes
- Flour
- oil
- Herbs
- salt
- pepper
- nutmeg

Preparation:

1. Whisk the 6 eggs together.
2. Line a tray with baking paper and pour the egg mixture on it and distribute it evenly.
3. Let the eggs set in the oven at 80 degrees until you have an even plate.
4. Chop the onions and fry them until translucent.
5. Add the mince to the onions and season everything with salt and pepper.
6. Fry the whole thing and deglaze it with the chopped fresh tomatoes and the strained tomatoes.

7. Taste the whole thing.

8. Let the meat steep.

9. Heat some oil and add the flour.

10. Mix the flour and deglaze it with the cream.

11. Season the flour mixture with salt, pepper, and nutmeg.

12. Add the crème fraîche and set aside.

13. Take the egg mixture out of the oven and cut it into slices.

14. Now stack the slices alternately with the minced meat mixture and the flour mixture in a baking dish. The flour mixture should form the top layer and then sprinkle the cheese on top.

15. Bake the whole thing in the oven for 20 minutes at 180 degrees, until the cheese has turned golden brown.

Zucchini spaghetti with Bolognese

Ingredients:

- 2 zucchini
- 1 finely chopped onion
- 500 g ground turkey
- 100 ml of milk
- 1 packet of strained tomatoes
- 3 tbsp tomato paste
- salt
- pepper
- oregano
- olive oil
- Freshly grated parmesan

Preparation:

1. Stew the onions in olive oil.

2. Add the hack.

3. Add the tomato paste and the strained tomatoes.

4. Bring everything to the boil and add the milk and a little salt.

5. Season the whole thing with pepper and oregano.

6. Let it simmer on low heat for 15 minutes.

7. Cut the pulp of the zucchini into strips.

8. Put the strips in a saucepan with a little salt and pour boiling water over them.

9. Let the zucchini steep for 5 minutes.

10. Take the minced turkey off the stove and pour off the zucchini strips.

11. Arrange the whole thing on a plate and sprinkle everything with the grated parmesan.

Sheep cheese on bed of vegetables

Ingredients:

- 1 onion
- 1 zucchini
- 1 bell pepper
- 400 g tomatoes
- 200 g feta
- Herbs

- Vegetable broth
- Balsamic vinegar
- garlic
- salt
- pepper

Preparation:

1. Cut the onions into rings and heat them in a pan with a little water until they are translucent.
2. Take a baking dish and add the sliced tomatoes, chopped peppers, and sliced zucchini.
3. Add the glassy onions.
4. Top it with the feta.
5. Mix the whole thing.
6. Prepare 50 ml of vegetable broth with garlic and balsamic vinegar and pour it over the vegetables and cheese.
7. Chop the herbs and sprinkle them on top.
8. Grill the whole thing for 15 to 20 minutes in the oven at 200 degrees.
9. Sprinkle everything with pepper and serve.

Low carb salmon with roasted vegetables

Ingredients:

- 2 cloves of garlic
- 1 zucchini
- 1 bell pepper
- 300 g cherry tomatoes
- 250 g salmon fillet
- 150 g mushrooms
- 100 g sheep cheese
- salt
- pepper
- Chili oil

Preparation:

1. Wash the fillet and dry it. Season it with salt, pepper and the herbs.
2. Cut the cheese into cubes.
3. Cut the zucchini and mushrooms into thin slices.
4. Cut the peppers into strips.
5. Quarter the tomatoes.
6. Chop the garlic.
7. Mix the vegetables with the garlic, salt and pepper, and some chili oil in a bowl.
8. Take a baking sheet and place a baking dish on it.
9. Spread the vegetables out in the pan.
10. Put the salmon on top and drizzle with the chili oil.
11. Put the cheese on top.
12. Cook the whole thing at 180 degrees for 30 to 35 minutes.

Zucchini - tuna pan

Ingredients:

- 1 zucchini
- 1 onion
- 1 can of tuna in its own juice
- 1 scoop of mozzarella
- 2 tbsp olive oil
- 2 tbsp cream cheese
- 1 tbsp balsamic vinegar
- Spice mix
- basil

Preparation:

1. Cut the zucchini into pieces.
2. Chop the onion and sweat it in olive oil in a pan.
3. Add the zucchini and let everything brown nicely.
4. Add the spice mixture.
5. Put the torn tuna in the pan without juice.
6. Add the cream cheese.
7. Cut the mozzarella into cubes, spread them on the tuna and let them melt.
8. Add the balsamic vinegar and taste the whole thing.

Grilled sheep's cheese with garlic tomatoes

Ingredients:

- 5 tomatoes
- 7 cloves of garlic
- 600 g sheep cheese
- 5 tbsp olive oil
- 1 bunch of basil
- salt
- pepper

Preparation:

1. Preheat the oven to 220 degrees and set it to convection.
2. Peel and mash the garlic and add it to the olive oil.
3. Cut the sheep's cheese into thick slices and put them in the baking dish.
4. Drizzle with the garlic oil.
5. Halve the tomatoes and place them on the cheese, cut side up.
6. Salt and pepper the whole thing and pour the remaining garlic oil over it.
7. Put everything in the oven and bake for 15 minutes.
8. Turn on the grill and grill everything until the cheese has turned lightly brown.
9. Pluck the basil, cut it into strips and sprinkle it over the grilled cheese before serving.

Doner pan with vegetables

Ingredients:

- 1 zucchini
- 1 leek stick
- 200 g seasoned poultry meat
- 50 g feta
- 2 tbsp crème légère
- salt
- pepper
- Paprika powder
- cumin

Preparation:

1. Clean the vegetables and cut them into small pieces.
2. Fry it with the meat in the pan.
3. Add the crème légère and the feta and season with spices.

Wrong rice

Ingredients:

- 700 g cauliflower
- 2 tbsp butter
- salt
- nutmeg

Preparation:

1. Clean, wash, and dry the cauliflower and divide it into florets.
2. Put the florets in a blender and chop them on a high setting.
3. Put it in a microwave-safe bowl.
4. Cook everything in the microwave for 5 to 8 minutes at full power.
5. Halfway through, give it a quick shake.
6. At the end add the butter and season everything with salt and nutmeg.

Tomato and zucchini pan with feta

Ingredients:

- 2 zucchini, washed and sliced
- 3 tomatoes cut into pieces
- 100 g diced feta
- 2 tbsp olive oil
- 2 sprigs of basil
- salt
- pepper

Preparation:

1. Put the olive oil in a pan and fry the zucchini slices, stirring occasionally.
2. Add the diced tomatoes and let them cook for 2 to 3 minutes.
3. Add the basil leaves and season everything with salt and pepper.
4. Add the cubes of feta and turn off the stove.
5. Let the feta melt through the residual heat and serve everything.

Minced meat pan with tomatoes and vegetables

Ingredients:

- 3 spring onions
- 3 cloves of garlic
- 2 tomatoes
- 1 zucchini
- 1 eggplant
- 1 mozzarella ball
- 1 can of pizza tomatoes
- 500 g ground beef
- 150 g cream cheese
- 2 tbsp olive oil
- salt
- pepper
- basil

Preparation:

1. Cut the onion into rings and squeeze the garlic.
2. Heat the olive oil in a pan and briefly sweat the onions and garlic in it.
3. Add the mince and fry it.
4. Cut the vegetables into cubes and the mozzarella into slices.
5. Add the diced vegetables to the minced meat and fry them briefly.
6. Add the pizza tomatoes and heat everything.
7. Pour the cream cheese over it and taste everything with the spices and herbs.
8. Finally, add the mozzarella to the vegetables and leave everything in the covered pan until the cheese melts.

Low carb puree

Ingredients:

- 500 g cauliflower
- 4 tbsp double cream cheese
- 1 tbsp butter
- salt
- pepper
- nutmeg

Preparation:

1. Divide the cauliflower into florets and soak it in well-salted water for 30 minutes.
2. Then cook the cauliflower in fresh, salted water for 15 minutes until it becomes soft.
3. Let it drain very well and puree it with a hand blender while it is still hot.
4. Mix everything with butter and cream cheese and season with salt, pepper and nutmeg.
5. Serve the whole thing while it's still warm.

Herb and tomato pan with juicy poultry meat

Ingredients:

- 1 onion
- 150 g poultry meat
- 100 g mushrooms
- 100 g cherry tomatoes
- 1 tbsp cream cheese
- 1 teaspoon Italian herbs
- 1 teaspoon chilli flakes
- salt
- pepper
- oil

Preparation:

1. Chop the meat, mushrooms, and tomatoes.
2. Fry the meat with a little oil and season it with salt, pepper and the chilli flakes.
3. Add the onions and mushrooms and cook for 3 to 4 minutes.
4. Add the remaining ingredients and stir everything.
5. Let the whole thing simmer gently for 5 minutes and then arrange it.

Thai soup with glass noodles, spinach and chicken

Ingredients:

- 2 chopped chili peppers
- 1 onion
- 1 can of coconut milk
- 500 g chicken breast fillet
- 500 g of washed spinach leaves
- 500 ml vegetable broth
- 1 packet of shirataki noodles
- salt
- pepper
- oil

Preparation:

1. Cut the meat into pieces and fry it in a large saucepan with a little oil.
2. Cut the onions into small cubes and fry them until translucent.
3. Pour in the coconut milk and let everything boil briefly.
4. Add the vegetable broth and let it boil again briefly.
5. Stir in the spinach leaves and season everything with salt and pepper.
6. Let it cook for 10 minutes.
7. Prepare the noodles according to the instructions and place them on a plate.
8. Pour the soup over the noodles and serve the whole thing.

Low carb pizza

Ingredients:

- 2 eggs
- 1 can of tuna
- 200 g of cottage cheese
- 3 tbsp bran
- 1 tbsp grated hard cheese

Preparation:

1. Preheat the oven to 180 degrees and set it to circulating air.
2. Drain the tuna and place it in a bowl with the other ingredients.
3. Mix everything smoothly with a fork.
4. Lay out the dough on a baking sheet lined with baking paper as a pizza.
5. Bake the bottom in the oven for 30 to 35 minutes.
6. Then top the dough with pizza sauce, sausage, vegetables, mozzarella, parmesan and anything else you like.

Zucchini and carrot ribbon noodles with chicken and tomato

Ingredients:

- 4 tomatoes
- 3 zucchini
- 2 carrots
- 500 g chicken breast fillet
- 150 g goat cream cheese
- 3 tablespoons water
- 3 tbsp tomato paste
- 2 tbsp olive oil
- 1 tsp red curry paste
- 1 teaspoon of broth
- salt
- pepper

Preparation:

1. Wash the chicken breast fillet, pat it dry, and cut it into pieces.
2. Heat the olive oil with the red curry paste in a non-stick pan and fry the meat on all sides until crispy.
3. Wash the zucchini and use a peeler to cut the ribbon noodles.
4. Peel the carrots and cut them into pasta as well.
5. Take the meat out of the pan, but leave the juice inside.
6. Add the noodles to the water and the broth with the cooking juice and bring them to the boil.
7. Cut the tomatoes into cubes and add them to the pasta with the tomato paste.
8. Add the cheese and meat and heat everything again, stirring constantly.
9. Season everything with salt and pepper and serve.

Salmon wrapped in bacon, with spicy stir-fried vegetables and feta cheese

Ingredients:

- 1 onion
- 125 g salmon fillet
- 100 g broccoli
- 100 g mushrooms
- 70 g zucchini
- 70 g feta
- 50 grams of bacon
- 10 g grated parmesan cheese
- salt
- pepper
- Chilli flakes
- Paprika powder
- olive oil

Preparation:

1. Wash the salmon, pat it dry, and wrap it completely in bacon.
2. Clean and cut the broccoli, mushrooms, onions, and zucchini.
3. Take a pan and add the oil.
4. Fry the salmon with the bacon and the prepared vegetables.
5. Season all of them with salt and pepper, the chilli flakes and the paprika powder.
6. Put a lid on and cook for 12 minutes.
7. Add the feta after 10 minutes.
8. At the end, sprinkle the parmesan on top.

Cauliflower with minced meat and bacon

Ingredients:

- 3 eggs
- 1 onion
- 1 cauliflower
- 1 kg mince
- 200 grams of bacon
- 50 g low-fat quark
- salt
- pepper
- mustard
- Caraway seed
- marjoram
- Paprika powder
- Diced bacon
- Grated cheese

Preparation:

1. Clean the cauliflower and cut the stalk crosswise.
2. Boil the whole thing in salted water for 10 minutes as it is.
3. Cut the onions into small cubes.
4. Season the mince with salt, pepper, mustard, caraway seeds, marjoram and paprika and mix it with the onions, bacon cubes, eggs and quark.
5. Drain the cauliflower and place it in a baking dish while it is still hot.
6. Cover the cauliflower evenly with the minced meat and then the bacon crusts so that the entire surface disappears.
7. Preheat the oven to 180 degrees and set it to top / bottom heat.
8. Bake the whole thing for 1 hour.

Low carb pizza roll

Ingredients:

For the dough:

- 3 eggs
- 120 g quark
- 120 g of grated cheese

Preparation:

1. Preheat the oven to 170 degrees.
2. Mix the quark, eggs and 120 g cheese in a bowl and season.
3. Line a baking sheet with parchment paper and pour the mixture on top. Smooth them out.
4. Bake the mass in the oven for 15 minutes.
5. Take out the bleach and cover the base with any tomato sauce, salami, ham and whatever you like and at the end sprinkle the 60 g cheese over it.
6. Put everything back in the oven and bake until the cheese is a nice color.
7. Let everything cool and top it with the rocket.
8. Roll it up and enjoy it.

Stuffed mushrooms

Ingredients:

- 8 large mushrooms
- 1 onion
- 1 cup of sour cream
- 80 g diced ham
- 80 g grated Gouda cheese
- ½ bunch of chives
- salt
- pepper
- butter
- oil

Preparation:

1. Clean the mushrooms and pull out the stems. Set the stems aside.
2. Dice the stalks of the mushrooms and the onion.
3. Cut the chives into rings.
4. Grease a baking dish and place the mushroom caps on top with the cook facing up.
5. Preheat the oven to 200 degrees.
6. Briefly fry the mushroom cubes and the onion with a little butter and oil together with the ham cubes in a pan.
7. Mix the onion, mushrooms, and ham mixture with the sour cream and chives.
8. Season the whole thing with salt and pepper.
9. Pour the mixture into the mushrooms.
10. Sprinkle the grated cheese on top and put the mushrooms in the oven.

11. Bake them for 15 to 20 minutes, until the cheese is lightly browned.

Zucchini Lasagna

Ingredients:

- 1 onion
- 1 clove of garlic
- 1 can of chopped tomatoes
- 1 kg of zucchini
- 500 g ground beef
- 150 g of grated cheese
- 100 ml of milk
- 1 packet of cream cheese
- 1 tbsp tomato paste
- sour cream
- olive oil
- oregano
- thyme
- parsley
- salt
- pepper
- Paprika powder

Preparation:

1. Cut the zucchini into slices.
2. Fry the slices in a pan with olive oil on both sides. Then let them drain.
3. Cut the onions into cubes and sauté them in the pan in olive oil.
4. Add the garlic clove and steam it with it.
5. Add the mince and fry it until crumbly.
6. Season the meat with salt, pepper, and paprika powder.
7. Add 1 tablespoon of tomato paste and stir it in.
8. Sweat everything on for a minute.
9. Add the tomatoes, oregano, some thyme, salt, pepper, and paprika powder.
10. Let everything simmer for 10 minutes on a low heat and add the chopped parsley at the end.
11. Mix the cream cheese with the milk and stir in the sour cream.
12. Season the mixture with salt, pepper, and nutmeg.
13. Stir in 50 grams of cheese.
14. Line a baking dish with the zucchini slices.
15. Put some of the tomato and mince sauce on top, then some of the cream cheese sauce and then again zucchini slices. Keep layering until all ingredients are used up.
16. The top layer should be the tomato mince sauce.
17. Sprinkle the rest of the cheese on top and bake everything for 30 minutes in the oven preheated to 200 degrees.

Low carb 'Labskaus'

Ingredients:

- 2 eggs
- 1 onion

- 1 jar of pickles
- 1 gals beetroot
- 1 can of corned beef
- 1 cauliflower
- salt
- pepper

Preparation:

1. Remove the stalk from the cauliflower and cook it in salted water until it is firm to the bite.
2. Cut the onions and pickles into small pieces.
3. Drain the cauliflower.
4. Meanwhile, braise the onions, pickles, corned beef in a saucepan and remove the liquid from the pickle jar.
5. Puree the cauliflower and add it to the mixture.
6. Add the juice of the beetroot.
7. Season everything with salt and pepper.
8. Fry a fried egg in another pan.
9. Put the Labskaus on a plate and add a few pickles and beetroot. On top of that comes the fried egg.

Catalan Seafood Pot

Ingredients:

- 1 onion
- 1 leek
- 1 clove of garlic
- 1 can of peeled tomatoes
- 1 can of saffron
- 250 g seafood
- 250 g fish fillet
- 100 ml dry white wine
- 2 tbsp dry cherry
- 1 tbsp olive oil
- 1 teaspoon chilli flakes
- salt
- pepper

Preparation:

1. Cut the onions into cubes.
2. Cut the leek into rings.
3. Chop the garlic.
4. Put some oil, garlic, onions and leek in a pan and sweat everything.
5. Chop the tomatoes and add them with the juice.
6. Pour on the white wine and stir in the seafood.
7. Season the whole thing with salt, pepper, saffron and chili flakes.
8. Cover and let everything simmer for 10 minutes, stirring occasionally.
9. Wash the fish fillet and dry it. Cut it into pieces and season with salt and pepper.
10. Add the sherry to the seafood and stir in the fish cubes.
11. Set the stove to the lowest setting. Let everything rest for 7 minutes.

Cucumber noodles with peanut sauce

Nutritional values: kcal: 229 Carbohydrates: 7 g Protein: 6 g Fat: 20 g

Ingredients:

- 2 large cucumbers
- ½ bunch of spring onions
- 1 carrot
- 1 lime
- 50 g roasted peanuts
- 4 tbsp oil
- 2 tbsp vinegar
- 1 tbsp peanut cream
- ¼ bunch of coriander
- salt
- pepper

Preparation:

1. Cut the cucumbers into thin strips, but save a quarter of them.
2. Peel and cut the carrots into strips.
3. Mix both with vinegar and peanut cream.
4. Beat in the oil and season with salt and pepper.
5. Chop the leaves of the coriander except for a few for later.
6. Cut the spring onions into thin rings.
7. Cut the lime into wedges.
8. Peel the rest of the cucumber and cut it into slices.
9. Mix the cucumber and carrot strips with the dressing and chopped coriander.
10. Top with the peanuts and add the cucumber slices, lime and coriander.
11. Serve the whole thing.

Spinach and shrimp casserole

Nutritional values: kcal: 567 Carbohydrates: 8 g Protein: 45 g Fat: 39 g

Ingredients:

- 4 eggs
- 1 onion
- 1 clove of garlic
- 1 kg frozen leaf spinach
- 500 g ready-to-cook frozen sea prawns
- 200 g whipped cream
- 100 g double cream cheese
- 100 g hard cheese
- 1 tbsp oil
- salt
- pepper

Preparation:

1. Rinse, defrost, and pat dry the shrimp.
2. Cut the onions into cubes and chop the garlic.
3. Heat 1 tablespoon of oil in a large saucepan with a lid and sauté the onions and garlic in it.
4. Add the spinach and 4 tablespoons of water.

5. Boil the whole thing up and then let it simmer according to the instructions on the packet.

6. Put the spinach in a colander and squeeze it out well. Then let it drain.

7. Mix together the cream, eggs, and cream cheese.

8. Season the mixture with salt and pepper.

9. Mix the whole thing mimicking the spinach and spread it in a baking dish.

10. Rub half of the cheese over it.

11. Place the shrimp on top of the cheese.

12. Top with the rest of the cheese.

13. Preheat the oven to 180 degrees and bake for 30 minutes.

Paprika pans with cinnamon

Nutritional values: kcal: 324 Carbohydrates: 11 g Protein: 21 g Fat: 20 g

Ingredients:

- 2 green chili peppers
- 2 green peppers
- 1 onion
- 4 cloves of garlic
- 2 cans of tomatoes
- 100 g young spinach leaves
- 2 pack Halloumi
- 3 tbsp harissa
- 3 tbsp tomato paste
- 2 tablespoons oil
- 2 tbsp agave syrup
- 1 cinnamon stick
- 3 stalks of parsley
- Ground cumin
- salt

Preparation:

1. Cut the chilli pepper into rings.

2. Cut the peppers into cubes.

3. Cut the onion into strips.

4. Chop the garlic.

5. Put oil in an ovenproof pan.

6. Add harissa, tomato paste, 2 teaspoons of caraway seeds and sweat everything for 2 minutes.

7. Add the chili, bell pepper, onion, and garlic and cook for another 5 minutes.

8. Add the tomatoes with their juice and mash them.

9. Add the cinnamon stick and agave syrup.

10. Boil the whole thing up, then let it simmer for 6 minutes.

11. Stir in the spinach and let it simmer for a minute.

12. Season the whole thing with salt.

13. Preheat the oven to 200 degrees and set it to circulating air.

14. Cut the halloumi into slices.

15. Put the slices on the vegetable mixture and sprinkle with the parsley.

16. Cook everything in the oven for 15 to 20 minutes, until the cheese turns golden brown.

Fluffy chicken fillets in orange sauce

Nutritional values: kcal: 432 Carbohydrates: 11 g Protein: 44 g Fat: 22 g

Ingredients:

- 4 chicken fillets
- 2 spring onions
- 2 oranges
- 1 cucumber
- 1 small, red chili pepper
- 150 g sour cream
- 5 tbsp olive oil
- 4 tbsp balsamic vinegar
- salt
- pepper
- sugar

Preparation:

1. Cut the cucumber into long, thin strips.
2. Cut the spring onions into rings.
3. Cut the chili pepper into rings.
4. Mix the vinegar with salt, pepper, sugar and 3 tablespoons of oil.
5. Mix the dressing with the cucumber, spring onions and chili.
6. Season the meat with salt and pepper and fry in 2 tablespoons of oil for 10 minutes.
7. Peel the oranges and remove the white skin.
8. Cut the fillets from the orange and squeeze the juice out of the separating membranes.
9. Add the juice and sour cream to the pan.
10. Boil the whole thing and season it with salt and pepper.
11. Add the orange fillets and heat them up.
12. Prepare the salad.

Mushroom cream fillet pan with cauliflower rice

Nutritional values: kcal: 570 Carbohydrates: 14 g Protein: 44 g Fat: 34 g

Ingredients:

- 2 peppers
- 8 shallots
- 1 kg of cauliflower
- 600 g pork tenderloin
- 500 g mushrooms
- 300 g whipped cream
- 2 tbsp clarified butter
- 2 tbsp olive oil
- 1 teaspoon vegetable stock
- 8 stalks of thyme
- salt
- pepper

Preparation:

1. Cut the fillet into cubes.
2. Cut the peppers into cubes.
3. Halve the shallots.
4. Halve the mushrooms.
5. Heat the clarified butter in a large pan and fry the meat vigorously on all sides.
6. Season it with salt and pepper and take it out.
7. Fry the mushrooms in the frying fat.
8. Fry the shallots and peppers for a moment.
9. Season again with salt and pepper.
10. Return the meat to the pan and mix well.
11. Rub the whole thing off with 250 ml of water and the cream.
12. Boil it, stir in the broth, and let it simmer for 8 to 10 minutes.
13. Season everything with salt and pepper.
14. Wash and grate the cauliflower off the stalk.
15. Blanch the cauliflower in salted boiling water for 1 to 2 minutes.
16. Pour the cauliflower into a colander and let it drain.
17. Put it back in the pot and mix it with olive oil and thyme.
18. Arrange the fillet pan and cauliflower rice.

Shakshuka and goat cheese

Nutritional values: kcal: 278 Carbohydrates: 11 g Protein: 18 g Fat: 19 g

Ingredients:

- 4 eggs
- 2 green peppers
- 1 onion
- 2 cloves of garlic
- 1 leek
- 150 g young spinach leaves
- 150 g goat cream cheese
- 200 ml vegetable stock
- 2 tbsp olive oil
- ½ bunch of flat-leaf parsley
- salt
- Cayenne pepper
- Ground cumin

Preparation:

1. Cut the onion and garlic into small cubes.
2. Also cut the bell pepper and leek into cubes or rings.
3. Prepare the spinach.
4. Preheat the oven to 180 degrees and fan-assisted.
5. Put the oil in an ovenproof pan and fry the onion, garlic, paprika and leek for 5 minutes.
6. Pour in the stock and let everything boil.
7. Add the spinach and let it collapse.

8. Season the whole thing with salt, pepper and cumin.

9. Make 4 hollows in the vegetables and crack an egg in each of them.

10. Let everything set in the hot oven for 8 to 10 minutes.

11. Take the whole thing out, sprinkle the goat cheese and chopped parsley on top and serve the whole thing.

Baked honey goat cheese on salad

Nutritional values: kcal: 698 Carbohydrates: 13 g Protein: 30 g Fat: 55 g

Ingredients:

- 1 ripe avocado
- 4 soft goat cheeses
- 4 stalks of dill, mint and lemon balm
- ½ radicchio
- 150 g baby salad mix
- 150 g raspberries
- 4 tbsp light balsamic vinegar
- 3 tbsp oil
- 3 tbsp pine nuts
- 1 tsp + 2 tbsp liquid honey
- ½ teaspoon mustard
- salt
- pepper

Preparation:

1. Clean, wash, and drain the lettuce.

2. Cut the radicchio into strips.

3. Wash the herbs, dry them, and pluck the leaves.

4. Pick and wash the raspberries.

5. Mash a third of the berries with a fork.

6. Mix the crushed berries with vinegar, 2 tablespoons of water, mustard, 1 teaspoon of honey, salt and pepper.

7. Take a baking sheet and line it with parchment paper.

8. Put the cheese on the tray.

9. Spread the pine nuts on the cheese.

10. Spread the honey on it.

11. Bake everything under the hot oven grill for 2 to 3 minutes.

12. Halve the avocado and remove the pulp. Cut it into slices.

13. Spread the prepared ingredients on the plate.

14. Sprinkle everything with the sauce.

15. Put the cheese on top.

Vegetable salad

Nutritional values: kcal: 519 Carbohydrates: 11 g Protein: 12 g Fat: 44 g

Ingredients:

- 2 avocados
- 1 pomegranate

- 1 head of broccoli
- The squeezed juice of 1 lemon
- 400 g small carrots
- 250 g of brown mushrooms
- 6 tbsp oil
- 1 bunch of basil
- 1 packet of mixed seeds
- salt
- pepper
- Brown sugar

Preparation:

1. Brush, wash, and cut the broccoli into small florets.
2. Cook it in boiling salted water for 8 minutes and then drain it off. Scour it off with cold water and drain it.
3. Cut the apple and carrots into thin slices.
4. Cut the avocado into slices.
5. Whisk the lemon juice with sugar, salt, and pepper. Add some oil.
6. Chop the basil and mix it with the dressing.
7. Taste the salad and serve it with the core mixture.

Oven frittata with spinach and ricotta

Nutritional values: kcal: 208 Carbohydrates: 5 g Protein: 19 g Fat: 12 g

Ingredients:

- 8 eggs
- 5 stalks of basil
- 300 g cherry tomatoes
- 100 g young spinach leaves
- 100 g ricotta
- salt
- pepper

Preparation:

1. Chop the spinach into small pieces.
2. Cut the tomatoes in half.
3. Chop the basil.
4. Preheat the oven to 200 degrees with convection and line a baking dish with baking paper.
5. Whisk the eggs and season them well with salt and pepper.
6. Stir in the spinach, tomatoes, and basil.
7. Pour the mixture into the mold.
8. Spread the ricotta in pieces on top.
9. Bake for 20 minutes.
10. Take the frittata out of the oven.
11. Take them out of the mold with the parchment paper and cut them into pieces.

Cold eggplant feta soup

Nutritional values: kcal: 221 Carbohydrates: 7 g Protein: 9 g Fat: 17 g

Ingredients:

- 1 red chilli pepper
- 1 clove of garlic
- 4 stalks of basil
- 600 g eggplant
- 150 g whole milk yogurt
- 125 g feta cheese
- 600 ml vegetable stock
- 5 tbsp olive oil
- salt
- pepper
- Pepper berries

Preparation:

1. Halve the eggplant lengthways and cut the pulp crosswise.
2. Season it with salt and pepper.
3. Drizzle it with 3 tablespoons of oil.
4. Place the halves on a baking sheet.
5. Preheat the oven to 200 degrees with convection.
6. Cook the eggplant for 45 minutes.
7. Take them out, let them cool, and use a spoon to loosen the pulp.
8. Clean the chili pepper, cut it lengthways and remove the seeds.
9. Chop them up.
10. Chop the garlic.
11. Heat 2 tablespoons of oil in a saucepan.
12. Braise the chili, garlic, and aubergine pulp in it.
13. Add the broth and season everything with salt and pepper.
14. Cover and let simmer for 15 minutes.
15. Then take the soup off the stove and let it cool for 30 minutes.
16. Then put them in the cold for 3 hours.
17. Wash the basil, shake it dry, and pluck the leaves off.
18. Crumble the feta.
19. Mix the yogurt with 50 g feta and the basil leaves.
20. Add everything to the soup and puree it.
21. Season the soup to taste and pour it into deep plates.
22. Sprinkle them with the remaining feta and pink pepper berries. Garnish with the rest of the basil.

Cauliflower kofte with red cabbage salad

Nutritional values: kcal: 390 Carbohydrates: 15 g Protein: 18 g Fat: 28 g

Ingredients:

- 2 eggs
- 1 cauliflower
- ½ cucumber
- 600 g red cabbage

- 200 g carrots
- 80 g mountain cheese
- 6 tbsp rapeseed oil
- 4 tbsp orange juice
- 2 tbsp ground almonds
- 2 tbsp fruit vinegar
- 4 teaspoons sweet and hot chili sauce
- 4 stalks of parsley
- salt
- pepper

Preparation:

1. Preheat the oven to 200 degrees and fan-assisted.
2. Line a baking sheet with parchment paper.
3. Brush, wash, and rub the cauliflower.
4. Spread it on the baking sheet and bake it in the oven for 10 to 15 minutes.
5. Take it out and let it cool down.
6. Clean, wash, and cut the red cabbage into thin strips.
7. Add ½ teaspoon salt to the red cabbage and knead the whole thing thoroughly.
8. Peel and grate the carrots.
9. Cut the cucumber into thin slices.
10. Mix the vinegar, orange juice and pepper.
11. Beat in 2 tablespoons of oil.
12. Add all the salad ingredients.
13. Grate the cheese.
14. Squeeze the cauliflower well on a tea towel.
15. Then knead it with the cheese, eggs and almonds.
16. Season the whole thing with salt and pepper.
17. Form small balls out of the mass.
18. Heat 4 tablespoons of oil in a pan.
19. Add the balls and cook on all sides for 8 minutes.
20. Put the finished Köfte in the oven to keep them warm at 100 degrees.
21. Chop the parsley.
22. Taste the salad again.
23. Arrange the köfte and pour the parsley and 1 teaspoon of chili sauce over it.

Stuffed eggplants

Nutritional values: kcal: 220 Carbohydrates: 10 g Protein: 5 g Fat: 17 g

Ingredients:

- 4 eggplants
- 4 tomatoes
- 2 onions
- 2 pointed peppers
- 4 cloves of garlic
- 6 tbsp olive oil
- 3 tbsp lemon juice
- 1 tbsp tomato paste

- 1 bunch of parsley
- salt
- pepper

- Ground cumin
- sugar

Preparation:

1. Wash the eggplant and peel the peel lengthways all around.
2. Cut the eggplant lengthways to the middle.
3. Put them in a bowl of salted water.
4. Add lemon juice.
5. Let the eggplant steep for 30 minutes.
6. Peel the onions and garlic.
7. Cut the onions into rings and the garlic into slices.
8. Clean the peppers and cut them into cubes.
9. Also cut the tomatoes into lumps.
10. Take the eggplants out of the water and pat them dry.
11. Heat 3 tablespoons of oil in a large pan.
12. Fry the aubergines all over for 7 minutes.
13. Take them out.
14. Heat 3 tablespoons of oil in the frying fat.
15. Sauté the onions and garlic in it until translucent.
16. Add the peppers and steam them for 5 minutes.
17. Stir in the tomato paste and diced tomatoes.
18. Pour in 100 ml of water.
19. Add salt, pepper and caraway seeds, and some sugar, and let everything simmer for 5 to 10 minutes.
20. Preheat the oven to 180 degrees and fan-assisted.
21. Put the eggplants in a baking dish.
22. Push them apart.
23. Add the vegetable mixture to the eggplant.
24. Put water in the mold.
25. Bake the eggplants for 30 to 40 minutes.
26. Chop the parsley and sprinkle it on top at the end.

Omelette with lentils

Nutritional values: kcal: 505 Carbohydrates: 11 g Protein: 26 g Fat: 39 g

Ingredients:

- 4 eggs
- ½ red chilli pepper

- 1 clove of garlic
- 100 g feta

- 50 g red lentils
- 4 tablespoons of milk
- 4 tbsp orange juice
- 4 tbsp water
- 2 tablespoons oil
- 2 tbsp white wine vinegar
- 1 tbsp oil
- 1 tbsp chili sauce
- 3 stalks of coriander
- salt
- pepper
- salt
- pepper

Preparation:

1. Whisk the eggs with the milk.
2. Season them with salt and pepper.
3. Heat oil in a pan and pour in the egg mixture.
4. Let everything stand on low heat for 5 minutes.
5. Turn the whole thing over and let it cook for 1 minute.
6. Take the omelette out of the pan.
7. Cut it in half and serve it.
8. Cut the half chili pepper into rings.
9. Chop the garlic.
10. Heat 1 tablespoon of oil in a saucepan.
11. Add the garlic and chili and sauté the whole thing.
12. Add 50 g of red lentils.
13. Quench the whole thing with 2 tablespoons of white wine vinegar, 4 tablespoons of orange juice and 4 tablespoons of water.
14. Cover and simmer for 8 minutes.
15. Prepare the omelette.
16. Chop 3 stalks of coriander.
17. Stir them under the lentils.
18. Season them with salt and pepper.
19. Place the lentil salad on top of the omelet halves.
20. Drizzle with the chili sauce.
21. Crumble the feta over it.

Zucchini cream soup with cream and Gorgonzola

Nutritional values: kcal: 305 Carbohydrates: 9 g Protein: 11 g Fat: 23 g

Ingredients:

- 4 zucchini
- 2 onions
- 2 cloves of garlic
- 150 g Gorgonzola cheese

- 100 g whipped cream
- 800 ml vegetable broth
- 2 tbsp olive oil
- salt
- pepper

Preparation:

1. Cut the zucchini, onions, and garlic into cubes.
2. Heat oil in a saucepan and sauté the onions and garlic until translucent.
3. Add the zucchini and steam them for 2 minutes.
4. Deglaze the whole thing with broth and let it simmer for 8 minutes.
5. Puree everything with a hand blender and season with salt and pepper.
6. Crumble the Gorgonzola.
7. Whip the cream until it is semi-stiff.
8. Serve the soup with the cream and the gorgonzola and sprinkle everything with pepper.

Cauliflower pizza with tomato and mozzarella

Nutritional values: kcal: 450 Carbohydrates: 11 g Protein: 31 g Fat: 32 g

Ingredients:

- 1 cauliflower
- 2 spring onions
- 1 onion
- 2 cloves of garlic
- 1 can of chopped tomatoes
- 300 g tomatoes
- 250 g mozzarella
- 200 g Gouda
- 2 tbsp olive oil
- 1 teaspoon dried oregano
- salt
- pepper
- sugar
- basil

Preparation:

1. Dice the tomatoes, onions and the garlic.
2. Heat oil in a saucepan and sauté the onions and garlic for 5 minutes.
3. Add the tomatoes and cook for 5 minutes, stirring constantly.
4. Season everything with salt, pepper, sugar and oregano.
5. Brush the cauliflower, cut it into large florets, and wash it.
6. Put the cauliflower in boiling salted water and blanch it for 4 minutes. Then pour it off and scare it off.
7. Cut the tomatoes into slices.
8. Cut the spring onions into rings.
9. Cut the mozzarella into slices.
10. Preheat the oven to 225 degrees and convection.
11. Coarsely grate the gouda.

12. Grate the cauliflower and mix it with the gouda.

13. Line two baking sheets with parchment paper.

14. Halve the cauliflower mixture and put it on each tray as a pizza crust.

15. Pre-bake them one by one in the oven for 10 minutes.

16. Put half of the tomato sauce, the tomatoes, spring onions and mozzarella on the first floor.

17. Finish baking it in the oven for 12 minutes.

18. Cover the second layer in the same way and finish baking it too.

19. Chop the basil and sprinkle it on the pizzas.

Omelette for two with ricotta

Nutritional values: kcal: 489 Carbohydrates: 8 g Protein: 34 g Fat: 33 g

Ingredients:

- 6 eggs
- 3 spring onions
- 1 red chilli pepper
- 250 g broccoli
- 100 g young spinach leaves
- 75 g ricotta
- 1 tbsp olive oil
- salt
- pepper

Preparation:

1. Clean, wash, and cut the broccoli into pieces.

2. Pick and wash the spinach.

3. Cook the broccoli in salted boiling water for 4 minutes. Add the spinach at the end and let it collapse.

4. Drain the vegetables.

5. Whisk the eggs and season with salt and pepper.

6. Cut the spring onions into small rings.

7. Chop the chili pepper.

8. Put the oil in an ovenproof pan with a lid.

9. Heat the oil and fry the spring onions and chili in it.

10. Add the broccoli and spinach.

11. Pour the egg in.

12. Cover everything and let it stand for 10 minutes.

13. Pour the ricotta on top and bake it under the grill for a moment.

Quick shakshuka

Nutritional values: kcal: 210 Carbohydrates: 11 g Protein: 11 g Fat: 12 g

Ingredients:

- 5 eggs
- 2 red peppers

- 1 onion
- 3 stalks of parsley
- 1 can of tomatoes
- 2 tablespoons oil
- 2 tbsp tomato paste
- 1 tbsp white wine vinegar
- salt
- pepper
- sugar
- Cayenne pepper
- Sweet paprika

Preparation:

1. Cut the pepper and onion into small cubes.
2. Put oil in an ovenproof pan and sauté both in it.
3. Add the tomato paste and sweat it on.
4. Pour in the tomatoes with their juice and 100 ml of water and let everything boil.
5. Season everything with vinegar, salt and pepper, 1 teaspoon sugar, ½ teaspoon cayenne pepper and 2 teaspoons paprika powder.
6. Cover and let simmer over low heat for 10 minutes.
7. Preheat the oven and set it to 175 degrees and convection.
8. Take the lid off the pan and beat an egg into it.
9. Put everything in the oven and bake for 5 to 10 minutes.
10. At the end, sprinkle the parsley on top.

Quick tomato and bean soup

Nutritional values: kcal: 190 Carbohydrates: 12 g Protein: 5 g Fat: 12 g

Ingredients:

- 1 onion
- 1 clove of garlic
- 1 bunch of soup greens
- 1 can of chunky tomatoes
- 1 can of white beans
- 300 g frozen green beans
- 4 tbsp olive oil
- 1 tbsp vegetable stock
- oregano
- salt
- pepper
- Rose peppers

Preparation:

1. Clean, peel and wash the soup greens.
2. Cut the leek into rings.
3. Cut the carrots and celery into cubes.
4. Cut the onion and garlic into cubes.
5. Heat oil in a saucepan.
6. Throw everything in and steam it.
7. Add the tomatoes and 1 liter of water and let everything simmer for 5 minutes.
8. Stir in the broth.

9. Rinse and drain the white beans in a colander.

10. Add the green beans and white beans to the soup.

11. Let everything continue to cook for 8 minutes.

12. Season everything with salt, pepper and paprika.

Salad with beetroot spirals

Nutritional values: kcal: 345 Carbohydrates: 9 g Protein: 9 g Fat: 29 g

Ingredients:

- 1 avocado
- 125 g baby salad mix
- 250 g beetroot
- 125 g blue cheese
- 6 tbsp oil
- 6 tbsp apple cider vinegar
- 1 tbsp liquid honey
- salt
- sugar
- pepper

Preparation:

1. Pick, wash and drain the lettuce well.
2. Clean and peel the beetroot.
3. Cut them into spaghetti.
4. Season them with salt and sugar.
5. Combine the vinegar, honey, salt, and pepper and whisk everything together.
6. Beat in some oil.
7. Halve the avocado, remove the pulp and cut it into slices.
8. Serve the salad with the avocado and beetroot.
9. Drizzle with the vinegar mixture and add the cheese.

Stuffed pointed peppers with chia seeds

Nutritional values: kcal: 280 Carbohydrates: 14 g Protein: 21 g Fat: 19 g

Ingredients:

- 4 red pointed peppers
- 1 bunch of spring onions
- 200 g sheep cheese
- Juice of 2 limes
- 2 tbsp chia seeds
- salt
- pepper
- Coarse pepper

Preparation:

1. Soak the chia seeds in 6 tablespoons of water for 10 minutes.
2. Wash, clean, and halve the peppers lengthways.
3. Cut the spring onions into rings.
4. Crumble the cheese.
5. Put the chia seeds in a colander and let them drain.

6. Mix the chia seeds with the sheep's cheese and spring onions.

7. Add lime juice, salt, and pepper.

8. Pour the mixture into the peppers.

9. Preheat the oven to 175 degrees and fan-assisted.

10. Add the peppers and bake for 12 minutes.

11. At the end, sprinkle them with the coarse pepper.

Tom Ka Tofu

Nutritional values: kcal: 324 Carbohydrates: 11 g Protein: 7 g Fat: 26 g

Ingredients:

- 6 spring onions
- 4 shallots
- 3 carrots
- 1 red chilli pepper
- 1 red pepper
- 1 bunch of coriander
- 5 frozen kaffir lime leaves
- 4 sticks of lemongrass
- 200 g tofu
- 150 g mushrooms
- 20 g ginger tuber
- 600 ml vegetable stock
- 400 ml coconut milk
- 3 tbsp oil
- 3 tbsp lime juice
- 1 teaspoon soy sauce
- ¼ teaspoon sugar
- salt

Preparation:

1. Let the lime leaves thaw briefly, wash them, and rub them dry.

2. Clean, wash, and pestle the lemongrass with a mortar.

3. Peel the ginger and cut it into slices.

4. Peel the shallots and cut them into small pieces.

5. Clean and halve the mushrooms.

6. Clean 2 spring onions and cut them into rings.

7. Wash and dry the chili pepper, then cut it into rings.

8. Wash and dry 6 stalks of coriander.

9. Put the stock, the lime leaves, the lemongrass, the ginger, the shallots, the mushrooms, the spring onions and the chili in a saucepan and cook everything.

10. Let it simmer for 10 to 15 minutes.

11. Cut the tofu into cubes.

12. Heat oil in a pan and fry the tofu for 4 minutes, turning it several times.

13. Deglaze the tofu with soy sauce and take it out.

14. Peel the carrots and cut them into strips.

15. Halve the peppers and cut them into cubes.

16. Clean the mushrooms and cut them into quarters.

17. Let the broth flow through a sieve into a second saucepan.

18. Put the lime leaves back in the pot.

19. Add the remaining rings of the chili pepper.

20. Pour on the coconut milk and boil the whole thing up.

21. Add the carrots, peppers, mushrooms and tofu and let everything simmer for 5 minutes.

22. Cut 4 spring onions into rings.

23. Season the soup with salt, sugar and lime juice.

24. Fill them into 4 deep plates.

25. Sprinkle them with the spring onions and garnish with the coriander.

Basic chili

Ingredients:

- 3 diced peppers
- 1 onion
- 2 cloves of garlic
- 2 cans of chopped tomatoes
- 1 can of corn
- 2 cups of red lentils
- 2 tbsp almond butter
- Vegetable broth

- Green beans
- salt
- pepper
- Cayenne pepper
- Paprika powder
- Chili powder
- oil
- Mexican spice mix

Preparation:

1. Add the red lentils to 4 cups of vegetable stock and cook for 10 minutes.
2. Fry the onion in another saucepan and add the diced paprika and green beans.
3. Add the peeled tomatoes and season everything with the vegetable stock powder.
4. Press the garlic in.
5. Add the corn and at the end the red lentils.
6. At the end, add 1 to 2 tablespoons of almond butter.

Vegetable pan with eggs

Nutritional values: kcal: 201 Carbohydrates: 9 g Protein: 11 g Fat: 11 g

Ingredients:

- 4 eggs
- 1 onion
- 2 cloves of garlic
- 1 bag of frozen vegetables
- 1 can of tomatoes
- 2 tbsp harissa paste

- 1 tbsp oil
- ½ teaspoon ground cumin
- salt
- pepper
- sugar

Preparation:

1. Cut the onion and garlic into small pieces.
2. Put oil in an ovenproof pan and heat it up.
3. Sauté the onion and garlic in it for 2 to 3 minutes.
4. Add the frozen vegetables and 2 tablespoons of water.
5. Boil the whole thing up, then let it simmer for 2 minutes.
6. Add the tomatoes, harissa, and cumin.
7. Let everything simmer for another 4 to 5 minutes.
8. Season everything with salt, sugar and pepper.
9. Beat the eggs and slide them into the pan.
10. Preheat the oven to 175 degrees and convection.
11. Put everything in and let it sit for 10 minutes.

Chickpea salad with tomatoes and cucumber

Nutritional values: kcal: 154 Carbohydrates: 11 g Protein: 2 g Fat: 11 g

Ingredients:

- 100 g tomatoes
- 60 g cucumber
- 50 g chickpeas
- 10 g green onion
- 1 tbsp olive oil
- salt
- pepper

Preparation:

1. Cut the tomatoes into pieces.
2. Cut the cucumber into pieces.
3. Cut the spring onion into rings.
4. Put everything in a salad bowl.
5. Add olive oil and season with salt and pepper.

Zucchini Chips

Nutritional values: kcal: 124 Carbohydrates: 2 g Protein: 1 g Fat: 3 g

Ingredients:

- 400 g zucchini
- 2 tbsp olive oil
- salt
- Paprika powder

Preparation:

1. Cut the zucchini into thin slices.

2. Line a baking sheet with parchment paper and place the slices on top. Make sure that the slices are individually, not on top of each other.

3. Let the slices steep for 5 minutes.

4. Dab the slices with a kitchen towel and brush them with olive oil.

5. Sprinkle them with paprika powder and salt them again.

6. Preheat the oven to 200 degrees and bake the slices in it for 8 to 12 minutes.

7. Let them cool down briefly and serve them.

Applesauce with cinnamon

Nutritional values: kcal: 92 Carbohydrates: 25 g Protein: 1 g Fat: 0 g

Ingredients:

- 1 kg of apples
- 1 cinnamon stick
- 1 star anise
- 250 ml of water
- 1 tbsp lemon juice
- Agave syrup

Preparation:

1. Cut the apples into pieces.

2. Boil them in a saucepan with water and lemon juice.

3. Add the cinnamon and star anise and cook the pieces covered for another 5 to 10 minutes.

4. Turn the apple pieces through the Lotte liquor.

5. Sweeten the whole thing with agave syrup and let it cool down.

Frittata with Spinach and Cream Cheese

Nutritional values: kcal: 338 Carbohydrates: 8 g Protein: 27 g Fat: 31 g

Ingredients:

- 4 eggs
- 100 g grainy cream cheese
- 50 g parmesan cheese
- 30 g raw spinach
- 3 tbsp whipped cream
- 1 tbsp olive oil
- salt
- pepper

Preparation:

1. Wash the spinach and let it dry off.

2. Beat the eggs and mix them with the whipped cream in a bowl.

3. Add the cream cheese and season with salt and pepper.

4. Heat the olive oil in a pan and add the egg mixture.

5. Add the spinach leaves and let everything set over medium heat.

6. Grate the parmesan and pour it over the omelette.

7. Preheat your oven to 180 degrees.

8. Put everything in the pan in the oven for 15 to 20 minutes at 180 degrees.

9. Take out the frittata and cut it into pieces.

10. Drizzle with lemon juice and serve whole.

Fried egg with green beans and peppers

Nutritional values: kcal: 356 Carbohydrates: 19 g Protein: 21 g Fat: 21 g

Ingredients:

- 2 eggs
- 1 shallot
- 150 g green beans
- 50 g red pepper
- 50 g Brussels sprouts
- 30 g peas
- 1 tbsp olive oil
- salt
- pepper

Preparation:

1. Clean the beans and cut them into pieces.
2. Cook them in a saucepan of boiling water for 5 to 6 minutes.
3. Take out the beans and let them drain.
4. Clean the Brussels sprouts and cut them in half.
5. Remove the peas from the pod.
6. Halve the peppers and cut out the seeds and dividers.
7. Cut the peppers into pieces.
8. Peel the shallot and cut it into cubes.
9. Heat the olive oil in a pan and sweat the shallot cubes in it.
10. Add the beans, Brussels sprouts, peas and bell pepper and sauté everything briefly.
11. Season everything with salt and pepper.
12. Beat the eggs in the center of the pan and fry them.
13. Then season them and serve the whole thing in the pan while still hot.

Chicken breast with stir-fried vegetables

Nutritional values: kcal: 381 Carbohydrates: 16 g Protein: 47 g Fat: 12 g

Ingredients:

- 180 g chicken breast
- 120 g diced carrots
- 120 g diced onions
- 80 g halved Brussels sprouts
- 1 tbsp olive oil
- salt
- pepper
- Chopped parsley

Preparation:

1. Wash the chicken breasts and drain them.
2. Heat the olive oil in a pan and fry the chicken breast until golden brown on both sides.
3. Season them with salt and pepper.

4. Put the vegetables in the pan and fry them.

5. Season everything again with salt and pepper.

6. Put everything on a plate and sprinkle with the parsley.

Beef steak with rocket and cherry tomatoes

Nutritional values: kcal: 434 Carbohydrates: 5 g Protein: 21 g Fat: 37 g

Ingredients:

- 1 beef steak hip
- 100 g halved cherry tomatoes
- 30 g butter
- 20 g rocket

- 1 tbsp olive oil
- rosemary
- salt
- pepper

Preparation:

1. Wash the beef and pat it dry.

2. Wash the rosemary and shake it dry.

3. Heat the butter and oil in a pan and add the beef steak along with the rosemary sprig.

4. Cook the steak for a few minutes, then turn it over.

5. Season it with salt and pepper and transfer it to a plate.

6. Meanwhile, wash and dry the arugula.

7. Break off the stalks that are too long and add the rest to the steak with the halved tomatoes.

8. Season everything with salt and pepper and serve.

Eggplant pizzas with tomatoes and basil

Nutritional values: kcal: 200 Carbohydrates: 6 g Protein: 7 g Fat: 15 g

Ingredients:

- 2 eggplants
- 1 bunch of basil

- 1 clove of garlic
- 300 g tomatoes

- 125 g mozzarella
- 4 tbsp olive oil
- oregano
- salt
- pepper

Preparation:

1. Clean the eggplants and remove the ends.
2. Cut the eggplant into slices and salt on both sides.
3. Wash the tomatoes, drain them, and cut them into pieces.
4. Wash and chop the basil. Put a few papers aside for later.
5. Mix oregano with olive oil in a bowl.
6. Cut the mozzarella into slices.
7. Add the tomatoes and basil to the oil mixture.
8. Mash the garlic and mix it in as well.
9. Season the whole thing with salt and pepper.
10. Line a baking sheet with parchment paper and place the aubergine slices on top.
11. Add the tomato mixture to the eggplant slices.
12. Preheat the oven to 175 degrees on top / bottom heat and let the pizzas bake for 10 to 15 minutes.
13. Take them out of the oven and place the basil leaves on top and serve everything.

Homemade meatloaf with cheese filling

Nutritional values: kcal: 472 Carbohydrates: 11 g Protein: 48 g Fat: 14 g

Ingredients:

- 1 onion
- 2 cloves of garlic
- 1 spelled roll
- 800 g minced veal
- 100 g diced Gouda cheese
- 100 ml of milk
- ½ bunch of parsley
- 2 tbsp yogurt
- 1 tbsp mustard
- nutmeg
- salt
- pepper

Preparation:

1. Put the mince in a bowl.
2. Pluck the buns small and soak them in milk in a bowl.
3. Cut the garlic and onion into cubes.
4. Chop the parsley.
5. Add the onions and garlic to the mince.
6. Take the bun out of the milk and squeeze it out. Add it to the mince with the yogurt and mustard.
7. Add some nutmeg, salt and pepper.

8. Knead everything with your hands.

9. Add the cheese cubes and the parsley and knead everything again.

10. Put the mince mixture in a loaf pan.

11. Preheat the oven to 220 degrees and add the mold.

12. Bake everything for 50 to 60 minutes.

13. Take the pan out of the oven, let everything cool for a few minutes and remove the roast from the pan.

14. Cut it into slices and serve it.

Chicken and Parma ham pan with basil sauce

Nutritional values: kcal: 411 Carbohydrates: 7 g Protein: 43 g Fat: 22 g

Ingredients:

- 1 onion
- 1 clove of garlic
- 4 chicken fillets
- 4 slices of Parma ham
- 400 g basil cream cheese
- 250 g cherry tomatoes
- 4 stalks of basil
- 2 tablespoons oil
- salt
- pepper

Preparation:

1. Cut the onion and garlic into cubes.

2. Wash and pat the fillets dry.

3. Wrap each fillet with 1 slice of ham.

4. Put the oil in a large pan and fry the fillets vigorously on all sides.

5. Take out the fillets.

6. Add the onion and garlic to the frying fat and sauté them.

7. Rub them in with 250 ml of water.

8. Stir in the cream cheese.

9. Season everything with salt and pepper.

10. Add the fillets and simmer everything for 10 minutes over medium heat.

11. Cut the tomatoes in half.

12. Pluck the basil into pieces.

13. Put the tomatoes in the pan and let everything simmer for another 2 to 3 minutes.

14. Season the sauce to taste and stir in the basil.

Medallions on tomato-chicory vegetables

Nutritional values: kcal: 405 Carbohydrates: 8 g Protein: 55 g Fat: 14 g

Ingredients:

- 8 pork medallions
- 4 chicory
- 1 can of chopped tomatoes
- 3 stalks of oregano
- 4 tbsp oil
- salt
- pepper
- sugar

Preparation:

1. Brush, wash, and halve the chicory lengthways.
2. Put 2 tablespoons of oil in a large pan and heat it up.
3. Fry the chicory in it for 4 minutes, turning.
4. Season everything with salt and pepper.
5. Take out the chicory and pour on the tomatoes.
6. Let them simmer gently for 5 minutes.
7. Season them with salt and pepper.
8. Add the chicory again and keep everything warm.
9. Wash the meat and pat it dry.
10. Tie the meat into the right shape with kitchen twine.
11. Heat 2 tablespoons of oil in a large pan and fry the meat for 10 minutes, turning it several times.
12. Season it with salt and pepper.
13. Arrange the chicory in tomato sauce, each with medallions, on plates and sprinkle with oregano.

Low carb pizza with zucchini crust

Nutritional values: kcal: 88 Carbohydrates: 3 g Protein: 7 g Fat: 6 g

Ingredients:

- 2 zucchini
- 1 egg
- 1 small onion
- 1 clove of garlic
- 150 g grated mozzarella
- 100 g cherry tomatoes
- 75 g grated parmesan
- 150 ml of pureed tomatoes
- 1 tbsp olive oil
- 3 stalks of basil
- 1 teaspoon tomato paste
- 1 teaspoon oregano
- salt
- pepper
- sugar

Preparation:

1. Cut the ends of the zucchini and grate the rest.
2. Mix them with a pinch of salt and let them steep for 10 minutes.
3. Then press the rasps out firmly and mix them with the egg, 50 g mozzarella and 50 g parmesan.
4. Form a pizza base out of the mass.

5. Line a baking sheet with baking paper and preheat the oven to 175 degrees with convection.

6. Place the pizza crust on the baking sheet and bake for 15 to 20 minutes.

7. Cut the tomatoes in half.

8. Cut the onion and garlic into cubes.

9. Heat oil in a pan and sauté the onion and garlic until translucent.

10. Add salt and tomato paste and rub everything off with the tomato paste.

11. Season the whole thing with salt, pepper and oregano and let it simmer for 5 minutes on low heat.

12. Take the pizza crust out of the oven, turn it and spread the tomato sauce on top.

13. Top it with 100 g mozzarella and bake it again for 10 to 15 minutes.

14. Take it out of the oven, pour the parmesan over it and sprinkle with the basil leaves.

Gratinated eggplant with salsicce

Nutritional values: kcal: 678 Carbohydrates: 9 g Protein: 29 g Fat: 58 g

Ingredients:

- 4 eggplants
- 4 tomatoes
- 1 onion
- 2 cloves of garlic
- 500 g salsicce
- 125 g mozzarella
- 5 tbsp olive oil
- 2 tbsp tomato paste
- 2 teaspoons of oregano
- salt
- pepper
- sugar

Preparation:

1. Clean the eggplants and cut them into 3 slices.

2. Season them with salt and set them aside.

3. Cut the tomatoes into cubes.

4. Cut the onion and garlic into cubes.

5. Take the skin off the bratwurst.

6. Heat 1 tablespoon of oil in a pan and fry the sausage in it.

7. Add the onions and garlic and fry them briefly.

8. Add the tomato paste and sweat it briefly.

9. Add the tomatoes and oregano and let everything simmer for 10 minutes over medium heat.

10. Season everything with salt and pepper.

11. Pat the eggplants dry and heat 4 tablespoons of oil in a pan.

12. Fry the eggplants on both sides and then let them drain on kitchen paper.

13. Put them on a baking sheet and spread the salsicce ragout over them.

14. Drain the mozzarella and grate it.

15. Put it on top of the eggplant.

16. Preheat the oven to 175 degrees and fan-assisted.

17. Bake everything for 10 minutes.

18. Take it out and serve the whole thing.

Tomato carpaccio with fresh yogurt cheese balls

Nutritional values: kcal: 280 Carbohydrates: 14 g Protein: 11 g Fat: 21 g

Ingredients:

- 1 red onion
- 1 clove of garlic
- 1 kg of mixed tomatoes
- 400 g yoghurt cream cheese
- 200 g watercress
- 60 g green olives
- 6 tbsp olive oil
- 2 tbsp lemon juice
- 2 tbsp chopped pistachio nuts
- 1 tbsp sesame seeds
- 1 tbsp sunflower seeds
- ½ bunch of coriander
- salt
- pepper
- Ground cumin

Preparation:

1. Chop the garlic and mix it with salt, pepper, juice and oil.
2. Briefly roast the sesame, sunflower seeds and pistachio nuts with ½ teaspoon salt and ½ teaspoon cumin.
3. Cut the tomatoes into slices.
4. Cut the onions into rings.
5. Pit the olives.
6. Mix everything with the watercress and coriander to make a dressing.
7. Scatter the seeds on top.
8. Serve the cheese in balls.

Pepper and tomato soup with Cabanossi

Nutritional values: kcal: 412 Carbohydrates: 12 g Protein: 21 g Fat: 30 g

Ingredients:

- 2 onions
- 1 red pepper
- 2 cloves of garlic
- 1 glass of roasted red pepper
- 1 can of tomatoes
- 200 g feta
- 150 g Cabanossi
- 2 tablespoons oil
- 1 tbsp tomato paste
- 1 tbsp vegetable stock
- salt
- pepper
- sugar
- Sweet paprika

Preparation:

1. Drain the roasted peppers.
2. Cut the onions and garlic into cubes.
3. Cut the cabanossi into slices.
4. Heat oil in a saucepan and briefly fry the Cabanossi in it.
5. Take them out and sauté the onions and garlic in the hot frying fat.
6. Stir in the tomato paste and sweat it briefly.
7. Extinguish everything with the tomatoes and their juice and 500 ml of water.
8. Add the roasted red pepper and broth.
9. Boil everything up and then let it simmer for 5 minutes.
10. Cut the fresh peppers into cubes.
11. Puree the soup with a hand blender.
12. Season everything with salt, pepper and paprika.
13. Heat the Cabanossi and the diced pepper in it.
14. Serve the soup and crumble the feta over it.

Zucchini mince pan

Nutritional values: kcal: 645 Carbohydrates: 11 g Protein: 44 g Fat: 51 g

Ingredients:

- 2 onions
- 2 small zucchini
- 1 clove of garlic
- 800 g mixed mince
- 300 ml of pureed tomatoes
- 5 tbsp olive oil
- 3 tbsp fried onions
- 1 tbsp soy sauce
- ½ teaspoon paprika powder
- 4 stalks of basil
- salt
- pepper

Preparation:

1. Cut the onions into cubes.
2. Chop the garlic.
3. Heat 2 tablespoons of oil in a large saucepan.
4. Stew the onions and garlic in it for 2 minutes.
5. Add the mince and fry it until crumbly.
6. Add the tomatoes and soy sauce and stir everything in.
7. Reduce the heat and let it simmer for 10 minutes.
8. Cut the zucchini into slices.
9. Heat the remaining oil in another pan and fry the slices in it for 1 to 2 minutes on each side.
10. Take out the slices and let them drain.
11. Wash the basil and pluck the leaves off.

12. Cut most of the leaves into small pieces.

13. Add the zucchini slices to the mince and stir in the shredded leaves.

14. Heat the whole thing.

15. Season it with salt, pepper, and paprika.

16. Garnish with the fried onions and the remaining basil and serve everything.

King oyster mushroom antipasti

Nutritional values: kcal: 289 Carbohydrates: 11 g Protein: 7 g Fat: 24 g

Ingredients:

- 6 king oyster mushrooms
- 2 cloves of garlic
- 4 slices of bacon
- 90 g baby salad mix
- 60 g baguette
- ½ bunch of chives
- 6 tbsp oil
- 4 tbsp balsamic vinegar
- 1 tbsp butter
- salt
- pepper

Preparation:

1. Chop the baguette into small pieces.

2. Chop the garlic and mix with 4 tablespoons of oil.

3. Clean the mushrooms and cut them into slices.

4. Prepare the salad.

5. Fry the bacon in a pan without fat until crispy.

6. Heat 1 tablespoon of garlic oil and butter in a pan and fry the bread in it until crispy.

7. Season the bread with salt and pepper and take it out of the pan.

8. Gradually add the mushroom slices to the pan and fry them with the remaining garlic oil.

9. Season them with salt and pepper.

10. Mix the vinegar, salt and pepper together and beat in 2 tablespoons of oil.

11. Cut the chives into rolls.

12. Crumble the bacon.

13. Serve the salad with mushrooms, croutons, and bacon.

14. Drizzle everything with the vinegar mixture and sprinkle with the chives.

Quick pan made from smoked pork and pointed cabbage

Nutritional values: kcal: 510 Carbohydrates: 12 g Protein: 35 g Fat: 32 g

Ingredients:

- 3 released Kassel chops
- 1 apple
- 4 stalks of parsley
- 600 g pointed cabbage

- 200 g carrots
- 200 g whipped cream
- 2 tablespoons oil
- 2 tbsp coarse mustard
- salt
- pepper

Preparation:

1. Cut the carrots into slices.
2. Cut the pointed cabbage into large pieces.
3. Pat the Kasseler dry and cut it into cubes.
4. Heat oil in a large pan and fry the carrots and smoked pork on all sides for 3 minutes.
5. Add the cabbage and the cream and cook the whole thing up. Then let it simmer for 5 minutes.
6. Cut the apple into small pieces.
7. Put the pieces in the pan and stir in the mustard.
8. Let everything continue to simmer and season with salt and pepper.
9. Sprinkle the chopped parsley on top and arrange everything.

Coconut and lime fish

Nutritional values: kcal: 441 Carbohydrates: 11 g Protein: 34 g Fat: 29 g

Ingredients:

- 2 spring onions
- 1 clove of garlic
- 1 piece of ginger
- 1 large red chili pepper
- 1 red pepper
- 1 lime
- 4 pieces of cod fillet
- 1 can of unsweetened coconut milk
- 5 stalks of coriander
- 3 tbsp oil
- salt
- pepper
- sugar

Preparation:

1. Chop the garlic and ginger.
2. Cut the chili pepper.
3. Cut the peppers into thin strips.
4. Cut the spring onions into rings.
5. Grate the peel of the lime.
6. Halve the lime and squeeze it out.
7. Rinse the fish and pat it dry.
8. Heat 2 tablespoons of oil in a large pan and fry the fish on each side for 2 minutes over medium heat.
9. Season the fish with salt and take it out.
10. Heat 1 tablespoon of oil in the frying fat and sauté the garlic, ginger, chili and paprika for 2 to 3 minutes.

11. Rub everything off with the coconut milk and 200 ml of water.

12. Season the whole thing with salt and pepper, boil it and add the fish.

13. Cover everything and let it simmer over low heat for 5 minutes.

14. Stir the spring onions and lime juice into the coconut sauce.

15. Season everything with salt and pepper and sprinkle with the coriander leaves.

Omelette with eggplant and tomato

Nutritional values: kcal: 417 Carbohydrates: 7 g Protein: 30 g Fat: 29 g

Ingredients:

- 4 eggs
- 100 g cherry tomatoes
- 50 g eggplant
- 1 stick of basil
- 1 tbsp whipped cream
- 1 teaspoon olive oil
- salt
- pepper

Preparation:

1. Cut the tomatoes and eggplant into slices.
2. Salt the eggplant a little.
3. Whisk the eggs with the cream and salt and pepper.
4. Heat oil in a pan and add the egg mixture.
5. Place the eggplant and tomatoes on top.
6. Cover the whole thing and let it all stall.
7. Season with salt and pepper and serve with basil.
8. Fold the omelette in half and transfer it to a plate.

Braised beef

Nutritional values: kcal: 275 Carbohydrates: 2 g Protein: 43 g Fat: 11 g

Ingredients:

- 3 cloves of garlic
- 800 g braised beef
- 400 ml beef stock
- 1 tbsp tomato paste
- 1 star anise
- 2 bay leaves, dried
- 6 sticks of thyme
- 1 tbsp olive oil
- 1 teaspoon shavings
- 1 teaspoon salt
- 1 teaspoon pepper

Preparation:

1. Wash the roast and cut it into cubes.
2. Press the garlic.
3. Heat the olive oil in the stew pan.
4. Add the beef, garlic, and thyme and sear the meat on all sides.

5. Add the tomato paste and fry it.

6. Fill the whole thing up with the stock.

7. Add the star corn, raselhanout, bay leaves, and salt and pepper.

8. Let everything simmer with the lid closed for 10 minutes.

9. Preheat the oven to 160 degrees.

10. Then put the closed pan in the oven and cook for 2 hours.

11. After an hour, take the pan out briefly and stir everything. Turn the meat as well.

12. At the end, take everything out of the oven, let it rest for a moment and arrange it.

Beef steak with broccoli

Nutritional values: kcal: 351 Carbohydrates: 6 g Protein: 29 g Fat: 22 g

Ingredients:

- ½ red onion
- 2 cloves of garlic
- 120 g beef fillet
- 60 g broccoli
- 30 g paprika
- 1 stick of basil
- 1 sprig of rosemary
- 2 tbsp olive oil
- salt
- pepper

Preparation:

1. Cut the peppers into strips.

2. Cut the onion into rings.

3. Chop the garlic.

4. Chop the herbs.

5. Wash the broccoli and remove the florets from the stem.

6. Cook the broccoli in water for 5 to 8 minutes.

7. Wash and pat the fillet dry.

8. Heat the olive oil in the pan.

9. Fry the fillet for 3 to 5 minutes on each side along with the rosemary.

10. Take out the fillet and season it with salt and pepper.

11. Add the peppers, onion, and garlic to the hot pan and sauté them.

12. Season them with salt and pepper.

13. Arrange the broccoli, stir-fried vegetables, and fillet on a plate.

14. Top with the basil and serve everything.

Celery puree with chives

Nutritional values: kcal: 86 Carbohydrates: 4 g Protein: 3 g Fat: 7 g

Ingredients:

- 1 celeriac
- 75 g soy cream

- ½ bunch of chives
- 1 tbsp olive oil
- nutmeg
- salt

Preparation:

1. Peel, clean, and cut the celery into cubes.
2. Put the celery in a saucepan and cover it with water. Cover and simmer for 15 to 20 minutes.
3. Drain the celery in a colander and let it evaporate in the empty, but still hot, pot.
4. Put the celery cubes in the blender jar.
5. Puree the celery.
6. Mix it with the soy cream, olive oil and salt and nutmeg.
7. Cut the chives into rolls.
8. Put the celery in a bowl and serve with the chives.

Raspberry tart

Nutritional values: kcal: 181 Carbohydrates: 2 g Protein: 5 g Fat: 9 g

Ingredients:

- 3 eggs
- 1 vanilla pod
- 250 g fresh raspberries
- 200 g almond flour
- 100 grams of erythritol
- 100 g butter
- 100 ml cream
- 2 tbsp raspberry jam

Preparation:

1. Put the butter, flour and half of the erythritol in a bowl and stir everything together.
2. Put the batter in a springform pan and spread the raspberry jam over it.
3. Cut the pulp from the vanilla pod, mix it with the rest of the erythritol, the cream and the eggs and add it to the batter.
4. Put the raspberries on the cake and bake it for 50 to 60 minutes at 160 degrees.

Blueberry-topped muffins

Nutritional values: kcal: 164 Carbohydrates: 3 g Protein: 2 g Fat: 9 g

Ingredients:

- 2 eggs
- 1 vanilla pod
- 150 blueberries
- 100 g almond flour
- 100 g butter
- 100 g whipped cream
- 50 g butter
- 50 g xucker
- 2 teaspoons of xucker
- ½ tsp baking powder
- Blueberry cream
- salt

Preparation:

1. Preheat the oven to 170 degrees and set it to circulating air.

2. Beat the butter with the xucker and a little salt until creamy.

3. Stir in the eggs one at a time.

4. Sieve the almond flour and baking powder and fold it into the butter mixture.

5. Grease the muffin cups and fill them two-thirds full with the batter.

6. Bake everything for 13 to 15 minutes.

7. Put some blueberries aside and puree the rest.

8. Sieve the pureed blueberries.

9. Bring the cream with the xucker and the pulp of the vanilla pod to the boil and add the puree.

10. Mix everything into a smooth mass.

11. Put the mixture on the butter and stir everything with the hand blender.

12. Let the cream sit for 4 to 5 hours at room temperature.

13. Mix the cream with a fork, pour it into a piping bag with a star nozzle, and pour it onto the muffins.

14. At the end, add the blueberries and serve everything.

Paleo apple muffins

Nutritional values: kcal: 122 Carbohydrates: 1 g Protein: 2 g Fat: 1 g

Ingredients:

- 8 eggs
- 3 apples
- 3 tbsp applesauce
- 3 tbsp honey
- 3 tbsp coconut milk
- 3 tbsp coconut flour
- 2 tbsp coconut oil
- 4 teaspoons of cinnamon
- 1 sachet of baking powder
- salt

Preparation:

1. Preheat the oven to 180 degrees.

2. Cut the apples into small pieces.

3. Fry two thirds of the apples in a pan with a little water for 5 minutes. Keep stirring the whole thing until it becomes a paste-like consistency.

4. Mix the eggs, applesauce, honey, coconut milk, and oil in a bowl.

5. Mix the coconut flour, cinnamon, baking powder, and some salt in a second bowl.

6. Now mix all the ingredients together and fold in the warm apples at the end.

7. Grease the muffin cups and pour in the batter evenly.

8. Press the remaining apple pieces onto the top of the dough.

9. Bake the muffins at 180 degrees for 30 to 40 minutes.

Chocolate shake with almond milk

Nutritional values: kcal: 351 Carbohydrates: 9 g Protein: 12 g Fat: 9 g

Ingredients:

- 300 ml almond milk
- 2 teaspoons of cocoa
- 2 tbsp maple syrup
- water

preparation

1. Put the almond milk with the cocoa and maple syrup in a blender and stir all the ingredients.
2. If necessary, add some more water and then enjoy it all.

Chia pudding with fruits and almonds

Nutritional values: kcal: 281 Carbohydrates: 15 g Protein: 6 g Fat: 17 g

Ingredients:

- 60 g strawberries
- 20 g blueberries
- 15 g chia seeds
- 150 ml almond milk
- 1 tbsp pomegranate seeds
- 1 tbsp almond flakes
- 1 tbsp coconut flakes
- 1 stick of mint
- Agave syrup

Preparation:

1. Combine the milk and chia seeds in a bowl.
2. Let them swell for 10 minutes.
3. Add the strawberries, blueberries, and mint.
4. Sweeten the pudding and add the pomegranate seeds, flaked almonds and coconut flakes.

Fruit salad with apricots and melon

Nutritional values: kcal: 143 Carbohydrates: 33 g Protein: 2 g Fat: 1 g

Ingredients:

- 4 apricots
- ½ apple
- 100 g melon
- 30 g strawberries
- 2 tbsp orange juice

Preparation:

1. Cut the apricots into pieces.
2. Quarter the strawberries.
3. Cut the apple into pieces.
4. Cut the melon into pieces.
5. Mix them together and serve.

Chocolate and cherry cake

Ingredients:

- 7 eggs
- 1 glass of sour cherries
- 200 g dark chocolate
- 10 g stevia
- 1 packet of custard powder
- salt

Preparation:

1. Separate the eggs and whip the egg whites with a little salt until stiff.
2. Melt the chocolate and let it cool a little.
3. Mix the egg yolks with stevia and stir in the chocolate.
4. Fold in the egg whites.
5. Bake everything for 30 minutes at 150 degrees on the fan.
6. Put the cherries in a saucepan with the juice and cook the whole thing.
7. Mix some of the juice with the pudding powder and add it to the cherries.
8. Mix everything and distribute the cherries on the cooled cake base.
9. Let everything sit in the refrigerator for an hour.

Quick raspberry ice cream

Ingredients:

- 200 g whipped cream
- 200 g frozen raspberries
- 2 tbsp almond butter

Preparation:

1. Put the cream in a tall container and stir in the almond butter.
2. Add the raspberries straight from the frozen food.
3. Chop the raspberries with a hand blender.
4. Mix everything well.

Chocolate brownies

Ingredients:

- 2 separate eggs
- 1 bottle of vanilla flavor
- 150 g xylitol
- 70 g almond flour
- 55 g butter
- 40 g cocoa powder
- 30 g dark chocolate
- 1 teaspoon stevia
- ½ tsp baking powder

Preparation:

1. Preheat the oven to 170 degrees.
2. Beat the egg whites into egg whites.
3. Break the chocolate into small pieces and melt them in the microwave with the butter.
4. Stir the cocoa powder into the butter mixture.
5. Mix in the remaining ingredients.

6. Fold in the egg whites.

7. Pour the batter into a brownie pan.

8. Smooth it out and bake it for 20 minutes at 170 degrees on top / bottom heat.

Low carb bars with almonds

Nutritional values: kcal: 111 Carbohydrates: 4 g Protein: 3 g Fat: 9 g

Ingredients:

- 40 g flaked almonds
- 30 g almonds
- 30 g butter
- 15 g of oatmeal
- 15 g ground almonds
- 10 g chia seeds
- 10 g coconut flakes
- 1 tbsp honey
- 1 tbsp agave syrup
- ½ teaspoon cinnamon
- ½ teaspoon ground bourbon vanilla
- salt

Preparation:

1. Put the butter, agave syrup, and honey in a saucepan and let everything melt over low heat.

2. Chop the almonds and add them to the saucepan with the cinnamon and vanilla.

3. Stir everything well.

4. Mash the flaked almonds and add them to the bowl.

5. Add the oat flakes and the ground almonds with the chia seeds, coconut flakes and a little salt.

6. Mix everything together and pour the mixture into a bowl.

7. Give them a good stir.

8. Line a baking sheet with parchment paper and pour the bar mixture on top.

9. Preheat the oven to 175 degrees and bake the mixture for 10 minutes.

10. Turn on the grill and grill everything for another 1 to 2 minutes.

11. Take the bleach out of the oven and let it cool down.

12. Then cut several smaller bars of the same size from one bar.

Low carb muffins with apple and raisins

Nutritional values: kcal: 312 Carbohydrates: 6 g Protein: 10 g Fat: 27 g

Ingredients:

- 4 eggs
- 1 apple
- 200 g ground almonds
- 100 g butter
- 2 tbsp raisins
- 4 tsp xylitol
- ½ teaspoon baking soda
- ½ teaspoon cinnamon
- salt

Preparation:

1.   Separate the eggs and beat the egg whites with a little salt until stiff.
2.   Grate the apple.
3.   Melt the butter in a saucepan over low heat.
4.   Mix the egg yolks with the xylitol, grated apple, liquid butter, baking soda, and cinnamon.
5.   Add the ground almonds and raisins and stir everything.
6.   Pull in the egg whites.
7.   Grease a muffin tin and divide the batter on it.
8.   Preheat the oven to 175 degrees and fan-assisted and bake everything for 20 to 25 minutes.
9.   Let the whole thing cool down before serving.

Low carb sub with guacamole and chicken

Nutritional values: kcal: 523 Carbohydrates: 9 g Protein: 7 g Fat: 6 g

Ingredients:

Sub:

- 3 cherry tomatoes
- 3 pickled green chillies
- 2 green olives
- 2 small mushrooms
- ½ red pepper
- ½ yellow pepper
- ½ cucumber
- Low carb baguette
- 1 chicken breast fillet
- salad
- salt
- pepper
- oregano

Guacamole:

- 2 spring onions
- 1 avocado
- 1 bunch of coriander
- ½ red chilli pepper
- Juice of a lime
- salt
- pepper

Preparation:

1.   Separate two to three stalks of coriander from the bunch and set them aside.
2.   Put the rest of the coriander in a food processor with the spring onions, the red chili pepper, the halved cherry tomatoes and the lime juice.
3.   Cut the avocado in half and remove the stone. Put the pulp in the food processor as well.
4.   Mix everything together and season with salt and pepper.
5.   Cut the lettuce into pieces.
6.   Cut the cherry tomatoes, olives, and mushrooms into small slices.
7.   Cut the peppers into thin strips.
8.   Cut the cucumber into thin slices.
9.   Roll the chicken breast fillet in salt, pepper, and oregano on a large sheet of parchment paper.

10. Wrap the paper and fold everything to a thickness of 5 cm.

11. Add everything to the pan and cook on each side for 3 to 4 minutes until golden brown.

12. Cut the baguette lengthways and brush it with the guacamole.

13. Then top it with the lettuce, bell pepper, mushrooms and cucumber.

14. Cut the meat into strips and add it to the bread as well.

15. Spread the cherry tomatoes and the rest of the coriander on top.

Satay tofu with broccolini

Nutritional values: kcal: 389 Carbohydrates: 14 g Protein: 25 g Fat: 25 g

Ingredients:

- 2 eggplants
- 1 onion
- 500 g broccolini or broccoli
- 300 g Chinese cabbage
- 300 g tofu
- 100 g peanut cream
- 3 tbsp oil
- 2 tbsp chili sauce
- 2 tbsp soy sauce
- ½ teaspoon sesame oil

Preparation:

1. Clean, wash, and chop the vegetables.
2. Cut the onions and tofu into strips.
3. Heat 2 tablespoons of oil.
4. Fry the tofu in the oil and take it out again.
5. Heat 1 tablespoon of oil in the frying fat.
6. Fry the eggplants in it. Take them out and fry the broccoli and onions in the frying fat for 2 to 3 minutes.

Hearty cauliflower cake

Nutritional values: kcal: 245 Carbohydrates: 11 g Protein: 13 g Fat: 14 g

Ingredients:

- 6 eggs
- 1 small cauliflower

- 1 onion
- 1 clove of garlic
- 1 small red and green bell pepper
- 150 g mountain cheese
- 100 g flour
- 3 tbsp oil
- ½ bunch of flat-leaf parsley
- salt
- pepper
- Fennel seeds

Preparation:

1. Clean the cauliflower, cut the florets from the stem, wash them and cut them into small pieces.
2. Cut the onion and bell pepper into short strips and chop the garlic.
3. Blanch the cauliflower in salted boiling water for 5 minutes, then drain and drain.
4. Heat oil in a pan and heat the peppers and onions in it for about 4 minutes, turning frequently.
5. Add 1 teaspoon of fennel and garlic and season everything with salt and pepper. Then let it cook for a minute.
6. Line a springform pan with baking paper and preheat the oven to 200 degrees with a fan.
7. Chop the parsley.
8. Grate the cheese.
9. In a large bowl, whisk the eggs together.
10. Mix in the flour, parsley, and two-thirds of the cheese.
11. Season the mixture with salt and pepper.
12. Fold in the cauliflower and paprika mixture.
13. Put the vegetable mixture in the mold and smooth everything out.
14. Top with the rest of the cheese and bake for 35 to 40 minutes, until the egg mixture has hardened.
15. Take the cake out and let it rest in the pan for 5 minutes.
16. Remove it from the mold and cut it into pieces.

Zucchini noodles with tofu sesame gröstl

Nutritional values: kcal: 335 Carbohydrates: 11 g Protein: 22 g Fat: 22 g

Ingredients:

- 1 kg of zucchini
- 1 piece of ginger
- 2 cloves of garlic
- 350 g smoked tofu
- 4 tbsp light soy sauce
- 4 tbsp fried onions
- 3 tbsp sunflower oil
- 2 tbsp sesame seeds
- salt
- pepper
- Juice of 1 lime

Preparation:

1. Cut the zucchini into long, thin strips.

2. Chop the ginger and garlic.

3. Crumble the tofu.

4. Put 1 tablespoon of oil in a large pan and fry the tofu for 2 minutes, turning constantly.

5. Add the ginger, garlic, and sesame seeds and cook for another 3 minutes.

6. Season the whole thing with soy sauce.

7. Take it out of the pan and keep it warm.

8. Wipe the pan with kitchen paper and then heat 2 tablespoons of oil in it.

9. Add the zucchini strips and steam them for 3 minutes, turning constantly, until they become firm to the bite.

10. Season them with salt, pepper and lime juice and serve with the tofumix.

Tomato and eggplant casserole with mozzarella

Nutritional values: kcal: 342 Carbohydrates: 8 g Protein: 19 g Fat: 24 g

Ingredients:

- 5 tomatoes
- 2 eggplants
- 6 stalks of thyme
- 3 cloves of garlic
- 250 g mozzarella
- 30 g parmesan cheese
- 5 tbsp olive oil
- salt
- pepper

Preparation:

1. Cut the eggplant into strips.

2. Gradually heat 5 tablespoons of oil in a pan.

3. Fry the aubergines in portions for 2 to 3 minutes per side until golden brown.

4. Take them out and let them drain on paper towels.

5. Wash the tomatoes and cut them into slices.

6. Cut the mozzarella into slices.

7. Cut the garlic into thin slices.

8. Preheat the oven to 200 degrees and fan-assisted.

9. Grease a baking dish and add the eggplant, tomato, and mozzarella alternately. Season each layer with thyme, garlic, salt and pepper.

10. Put the mozzarella on top as the top layer.

11. Bake for 30 minutes.

12. Grate the parmesan and pour it over the casserole 10 minutes before the end of cooking.

13. At the end, take out the casserole.

14. Garnish with the rest of the thyme and serve the whole thing.

Super delicious cauliflower soup

Nutritional values: kcal: 265 Carbohydrates: 11 g Protein: 9 g Fat: 21 g

Ingredients:

- 1 lemon
- 1 large cauliflower
- 2 cans of chickpeas
- 150 g Greek yogurt
- 50 g baby spinach
- 6 tbsp olive oil
- 1 teaspoon vegetable stock
- Curry powder
- Ground coriander
- salt
- pepper

Preparation:

1. Preheat the oven to 200 degrees and fan-assisted.
2. Line a baking sheet with parchment paper.
3. Let the chickpeas dry off.
4. Clean the cauliflower and cut it into florets.
5. Mix both with oil, 3 tablespoons curry and ½ teaspoon coriander as well as some salt and pepper and spread it on the baking sheet.
6. Put the whole thing in the oven and bake for 25 to 30 minutes.
7. Set aside a quarter of the mix.
8. Put the rest with 1½ l of water in a large saucepan and boil it up.
9. Stir in the broth and let the soup simmer covered for 5 minutes.
10. Prepare the spinach and puree the soup.
11. Season everything with salt, pepper and lemon juice.
12. Add the rest of the cauliflower mix to the soup and cook everything together for a moment.
13. Then serve the soup with the yogurt and spinach.

Turkey medallions alla Caprese

Nutritional values: kcal: 345 Carbohydrates: 2 g Protein: 44 g Fat: 19 g

Ingredients:

- 2 tomatoes
- 3 stalks of basil
- 500 g turkey breast
- 250 g mozzarella
- 2 tablespoons oil
- 3 tsp pesto
- salt
- pepper

Preparation:

1. Wash the meat, pat dry, and cut into medallions.
2. Cut the mozzarella into slices.

3. Cut the tomatoes into slices.
4. Pluck the leaves from the basil.
5. Heat oil in a pan and fry the meat all over for 2 minutes.
6. Season it with salt and pepper.
7. Spread the pesto in the pan.
8. Top the meat with basil, a slice of mozzarella and a tomato.
9. Cover and cook for another 5 to 6 minutes.
10. Prepare everything with the pesto sauce set.

Quick beans and fried eggs

Nutritional values: kcal: 354 Carbohydrates: 12 g Protein: 16 g Fat: 25 g

Ingredients:

- 4 eggs
- 1 onion
- 2 cloves of garlic
- 1 can of chunky tomatoes
- 1 can "Texas Mix"
- 80 g grated Gouda cheese
- 3 tbsp oil
- 1 tbsp tomato paste
- 4 stalks of parsley
- salt
- Chili powder

Preparation:

1. Cut the onion and garlic into cubes.
2. Heat 2 tablespoons of oil in a pan and steam both in it.
3. Stir in the tomato paste and sweat everything briefly.
4. Add 200 ml of water and the tomatoes and the drained Texas mix.
5. Season the whole thing with salt and chilli.
6. Boil it and let it simmer for 5 to 7 minutes.
7. Chop the parsley.
8. Heat 1 tablespoon of oil in a large pan and fry the eggs to make fried eggs.
9. Season them with salt and sprinkle cheese over them.
10. Let the cheese melt briefly.
11. Arrange the tomato and bean sauce with the eggs and sprinkle with parsley.

Chicken curry

Nutritional values: kcal: 365 Carbohydrates: 6 g Protein: 33 g Fat: 25 g

Ingredients:

- 3 tomatoes
- 1 onion
- 1 clove of garlic
- 1 can of creamy coconut milk
- 500 g chicken fillet
- 250 g young spinach

- 2 tablespoons oil
- 2 tbsp curry powder
- salt
- pepper

Preparation:

1. Cut the onions into cubes.
2. Press the garlic.
3. Cut the tomatoes into cubes.
4. Wash the meat, pat it dry, and cut it into cubes.
5. Fry the meat on all sides in a pan with oil for 4 to 5 minutes.
6. Add the onions and garlic.
7. Continue frying everything and after 2 minutes add the curry.
8. Add the tomatoes and continue cooking for 3 to 4 minutes.
9. Deglaze the whole thing with the coconut milk and let it simmer for 10 minutes.
10. Add the spinach to the chicken and let it collapse.
11. Season everything with salt and pepper.

Classic scrambled eggs with chives

Nutritional values: kcal: 156 Carbohydrates: 1 g Protein: 11 g Fat: 12 g

Ingredients:

- 6 eggs
- 1 bunch of chives
- 20 g butter or margarine
- 4 tablespoons of milk
- salt
- pepper

Preparation:

1. Cut the chives into rolls.
2. Whisk it with the eggs and milk.
3. Season the whole thing with salt and pepper.
4. Heat oil in a pan and bring the eggs to congeal while stirring slowly.

Stuffed peppers with turkey

Nutritional values: kcal: 180 Carbohydrates: 6 g Protein: 22 g Fat: 8 g

Ingredients:

- ½ bag of ready-made sauerkraut
- ½ red pepper
- 1 stalk of parsley
- 75 g turkey schnitzel
- 2 tbsp yogurt
- 1 teaspoon oil
- ½ teaspoon mustard
- salt
- pepper
- Sweet paprika

Preparation:

1. Cut the meat into cubes.

2. Drain the sauerkraut.

3. Cut the parsley into strips.

4. Mix together the yogurt and mustard and season with salt and pepper.

5. Fry the peppers on all sides in a little oil for 1 to 2 minutes.

6. Take out the peppers and keep them warm.

7. Put the turkey in the pan and cook for 2 to 3 minutes.

8. Season the turkey with salt, pepper, and paprika powder.

9. Add the sauerkraut and heat everything for 3 minutes.

10. Put the turkey meat and the sauerkraut in the warm pepper halves and top with the mustard cream.

11. Sprinkle everything with parsley and paprika powder.

Avocado salad with prawns

Nutritional values: kcal: 495 Carbohydrates: 7 g Protein: 21 g Fat: 42 g

Ingredients:

- 2 avocados
- 2 shallots
- ½ lettuce
- 400 g cooked prawns (without intestines, head and shell)
- 200 g cherry tomatoes
- 6 tbsp oil
- 4 tbsp balsamic vinegar
- 3 tbsp lemon juice
- 1 teaspoon honey
- salt
- pepper
- sugar

Preparation:

1. Wash the shrimp and pat them dry.

2. Cut the avocado into slices.

3. Mix the avocado slices with lemon juice.

4. Cut the tomatoes in half.

5. Chop up the lettuce.

6. Cut the shallots into cubes.

7. Whisk the vinegar with the honey and season the mixture with salt and pepper. Then beat in 5 tablespoons of oil.

8. Stir the shallots into the mixture.

9. Add 1 tablespoon of oil to the pan and fry the shrimp for 1 to 2 minutes on all sides and season with salt and pepper. Take them out afterwards.

10. Add the vinaigrette, cherries, shrimp, and salad to the avocado.

11. Mix everything, taste it and serve it.

Omelette with toasted mushrooms

Nutritional values: kcal: 236 Carbohydrates: 1 g Protein: 18 g Fat: 20 g

Ingredients:

- 8 eggs
- 200 g mushrooms
- 5 tbsp milk
- 2 tbsp olive oil
- 2 tsp turmeric paste
- 6 stalks of coriander
- Paprika powder
- salt

Preparation:

1. Preheat the oven to 220 degrees and fan-assisted.
2. Chop the mushrooms.
3. Whisk the eggs, milk, turmeric paste, and ½ teaspoon paprika powder and salt.
4. Chop the coriander and add three quarters of it to the egg mixture. Give the whole thing a good stir.
5. Heat oil in an ovenproof pan and fry the mushrooms on all sides for 2 minutes over high heat.
6. Pour the egg mixture over it.
7. Fry everything for another 3 minutes over medium heat.
8. Put everything in the oven and cook there for 3 to 5 minutes.
9. Then sprinkle everything with the rest of the coriander and serve.

Zucchini pasta with cherry tomatoes and pesto

Nutritional values: kcal: 251 Carbohydrates: 5 g Protein: 7 g Fat: 22 g

Ingredients:

- 1 pot of basil
- 1 clove of garlic
- 600 g zucchini
- 150 g red and yellow cherry tomatoes
- 50 g parmesan cheese
- 75 ml of olive oil
- salt
- pepper

Preparation:

1. Pluck the basil leaves.
2. Chop the garlic.
3. Grate the parmesan.
4. Puree the basil leaves, parmesan, garlic and olive oil together.
5. Season the mixture with salt and pepper.
6. Cut the zucchini into long strips.
7. Cut the tomatoes in half.

8. Mix the zucchini noodles and pesto.

9. Taste both.

10. Fold in the tomato halves and arrange everything on a platter.

Broccoli with ham and parmesan

Nutritional values: kcal: 202 Carbohydrates: 8 g Protein: 22 g Fat: 8 g

Ingredients:

- 2 heads of broccoli
- 1 onion
- 225 g cooked ham
- 75 g grated parmesan cheese
- 60 ml chicken broth
- 1 tbsp oil
- salt
- pepper

Preparation:

1. Chop the broccoli into small pieces also cut the stems into strips.

2. Cut the onion into cubes and the ham into pieces.

3. Heat oil in a pan and fry the onion and ham in it for 3 minutes on all sides.

4. Add the broccoli and broth and mix everything together.

5. Let the whole thing simmer for 2 minutes and season with salt and pepper.

6. Arrange everything on plates and sprinkle with parmesan.

Paprika and parmesan scrambled eggs with sausages

Nutritional values: kcal: 605 Carbohydrates: 3 g Protein: 32 g Fat: 54 g

Ingredients:

- 12 Nuremberg grilled sausages
- 8 eggs
- 1 glass of roasted red bell pepper
- 60 g grated parmesan cheese
- 5 tbsp whipped cream
- 3 tbsp oil
- salt
- Grated nutmeg

Preparation:

1. Cut the peppers into strips.

2. Whisk the eggs with cream and 40 g parmesan.

3. Season the mixture with salt and nutmeg.

4. Heat 2 tablespoons of oil in a pan and fry the sausages on all sides for 5 minutes.

5. Heat 1 tablespoon of oil in another pan and pour in the EGG.

6. Spread the peppers on top.

7. As soon as the one begins to stagnate, push it together but don't stir it.

8. Let the eggs set on a mild heat and don't turn them.

9. Sprinkle the rest of the parmesan on the egg mixture and serve with the sausages.

Cheese omelette with bell pepper curd

Nutritional values: kcal: 380 Carbohydrates: 3 g Protein: 26 g Fat: 31 g

Ingredients:

- 8 eggs
- 1 small onion
- 1 clove of garlic
- 250 g young spinach leaves
- 60 g parmesan cheese
- 3 tbsp oil
- 1 packet of paprika curd
- salt
- pepper
- Grated nutmeg

Preparation:

1. Cut the onion into cubes.
2. Chop the garlic.
3. Heat 1 tablespoon of oil in a saucepan and sauté the onions and garlic for 1 to 2 minutes.
4. Add the spinach.
5. Let the spinach collapse and season with salt, pepper, and nutmeg.
6. Put the spinach in a colander and let it drain.
7. Grate the parmesan.
8. Separate the eggs.
9. Beat the egg whites until stiff.
10. First fold in the egg yolks, then 50 g Parmesan, then the spinach and finally the egg white.
11. Season everything with salt and pepper.
12. Heat 2 tablespoons of oil in an ovenproof pan.
13. Fill in the egg mixture and let it set slightly for 3 minutes.
14. Put the remaining cheese on top of the omelette.
15. Preheat the oven to 200 degrees and fan- assisted.
16. Put the omelette in the oven and let it set for 10 minutes.
17. Season the quark with pepper.
18. Take the omelette out of the oven and serve immediately.
19. Serve with the curd.

Leaf salad with fresh figs and meat

Nutritional values: kcal: 475 Carbohydrates: 12 g Protein: 32 g Fat: 34 g

Ingredients:

- 6 figs
- 1 lettuce
- 250 g mozzarella
- 150 g Bündner meat in wafer-thin slices
- 50 g baby salad mix
- 4 tbsp balsamic vinegar
- 4 tbsp oil
- salt

- pepper
- sugar

Preparation:

1. Cut the lettuce into pieces.
2. Cut the mozzarella into pieces.
3. Remove the stems from the figs.
4. Cut the fruit into quarters.
5. Mix the vinegar with salt, pepper, and sugar. Beat in some oil.
6. Mix the salads with the figs, mozzarella and vinaigrette.
7. Put the meat on the salad.

Spinach and mushroom omelette

Nutritional values: kcal: 330 Carbohydrates: 2 g Protein: 20 g Fat: 27 g

Ingredients:

- 4 eggs
- 100 g mushrooms
- 30 g mozzarella
- 25 g baby spinach leaves
- 4 tbsp whipped cream
- 1 tbsp oil
- salt
- pepper
- Grated nutmeg

Preparation:

1. Cut the mushrooms into quarters.
2. In a bowl, whisk the eggs and cream together.
3. Season to taste with salt, pepper and nutmeg.
4. Heat oil in a pan and fry the mushrooms in it for 4 minutes.
5. Add the spinach.
6. Pour the cream mixture over it and let everything set for 7 to 8 minutes over low heat.
7. Cut the mozzarella into pieces and pour it over 2 minutes before the end of the cooking time and let it melt.

Quick Coconut Shrimp Curry

Nutritional values: kcal: 276 Carbohydrates: 5 g Protein: 19 g Fat: 19 g

Ingredients:

- 1 red chilli pepper
- 1 lime
- 1 can of unsweetened coconut milk
- ¼ pot of coriander
- 400 g prawns (without head and shell)
- 200 g cherry tomatoes
- 1 tbsp oil
- curry
- salt
- sugar

Preparation:

1. Cut the tomatoes in half.
2. Rinse the shrimp and pat them dry.
3. Finely chop the chili.
4. Heat the chili and 2 teaspoons of curry with a little oil in a saucepan and let it simmer briefly.
5. Pour in the coconut milk and 1/8 l of water.
6. Boil everything and season with ½ teaspoon salt and 1 teaspoon sugar.
7. Add the shrimp and tomatoes and let them simmer for 5 minutes.
8. Chop the coriander.
9. Squeeze the lime.
10. Season the curry with salt and lime juice.
11. Sprinkle everything with coriander.

Gratinated schnitzel with camembert

Nutritional values: kcal: 389 Carbohydrates: 14 g Protein: 36 g Fat: 17 g

Ingredients:

- 2 thick turkey schnitzel
- 1 pear
- 150 g camembert
- 1 tbsp oil
- 4 tsp cranberries
- 1 teaspoon butter
- salt
- pepper

Preparation:

1. Preheat an oven to 200 degrees and fan-assisted.
2. Wash the cutlets, pat them dry and cut them in half.
3. Fry them in hot oil for 3 minutes on each side.
4. Season them with salt and pepper and take them out.
5. Cut the cheese into slices.
6. Cut the pear into slices.
7. Heat butter in a pan and sauté the pear for 2 minutes.
8. Put the pear in a baking dish and pour the schnitzel and cheese over it.
9. Bake everything for 5 to 7 minutes and then serve with cranberries.

Ragout with salmon

Nutritional values: kcal: 444 Carbohydrates: 8 g Protein: 29 g Fat: 33 g

Ingredients:

- 1 onion
- 4 stalks of dill
- 2 kg of cucumber
- 500 g salmon fillet
- 150 g horseradish cream cheese
- 3 tbsp oil

- 2 tbsp light sauce thickener
- 1 teaspoon vegetable stock
- salt
- pepper

Preparation:

1. Cut the fish into cubes.
2. Heat 2 tablespoons of oil in a pan and fry the fish in it for 5 minutes.
3. Peel the cucumbers and cut them into slices.
4. Cut the onions into cubes.
5. Season the salmon with salt and take it out.
6. Heat 1 tablespoon of oil in the frying fat.
7. Fry the cucumbers and onions in it.
8. Stir in the broth, 250 ml of water, and the cream cheese.
9. Boil the whole thing up and let it simmer for 5 to 7 minutes.
10. Thicken everything with sauce thickener.
11. Season the whole thing with salt and pepper.
12. Chop the dill and fold it with the salmon under the cucumbers.

Quick, sweet salad with pear, pomegranate and nuts

Nutritional values: kcal: 229 Carbohydrates: 19 g Protein: 4 g Fat: 15 g

Ingredients:

- 100 g pear
- 30 pomegranate seeds
- 20 g walnuts
- 5 g baby spinach

Preparation:

1. Clean and dry the pear.
2. Cut it in half and cut out the core.
3. Cut them into thin slices.
4. Wash and drain the spinach.
5. Chop the nuts.
6. Alternate between pear, spinach, stone, and walnuts in a glass.

Orange-carrot power drink

Nutritional values: kcal: 115 Carbohydrates: 28 g Protein: 2 g Fat: 0 g

Ingredients:

- 1 orange
- 1 carrot
- 50 g apple
- 1 g grated ginger
- 100 ml of water
- Ground cinnamon

Preparation:

1. Halve the orange and squeeze it out.
2. Peel the carrot and cut it into pieces.
3. Wash the apple and cut it into pieces.
4. Peel the ginger and cut it into small pieces.
5. Put everything with the cinnamon and water in a mixing vessel and mix it to a puree.
6. Put the whole thing in a glass and enjoy.

Coleslaw with mint and lime juice

Nutritional values: kcal: 98 Carbohydrates: 14 g Protein: 2 g Fat: 1 g

Ingredients:

- Juice of a lime
- 4 stalks of mint
- 400 g Chinese cabbage
- 250 g carrots
- 2 teaspoons agave syrup

Preparation:

1. Remove the outer leaves of the cabbage.
2. Cut it into strips.
3. Peel and slice the carrot.
4. Wash the mint, shake it dry, and cut it into strips.
5. Mix everything together with the lime juice and taste with the agave syrup.

15-minute soup with zucchini and toasted bread

Nutritional values: kcal: 136 Carbohydrates: 12 g Protein: 4 g Fat: 9 g

Ingredients:

- 2 zucchini
- 1 onion
- 1 clove of garlic
- 2 slices of farmer's bread
- 1 glass of vegetable stock
- 100 g whipped cream
- 2 tbsp olive oil
- salt
- pepper
- Lemon juice
- cress

Preparation:

1. Cut the zucchini and onion into cubes.
2. Put 1 tablespoon of oil in a saucepan and sauté the zucchini and onion.
3. Add the stock and let everything simmer for 5 minutes.
4. Cut the garlic into thin slices.

5. Heat 1 tablespoon of oil in a pan and toast the bread and garlic in it.

6. Puree the zucchini in the stock.

7. Pour the cream into the puree and boil the whole thing up.

8. Season the whole thing with salt, pepper and lemon juice.

9. Serve the soup with bread and sprinkle the cress on top.

Lettuce hearts filled with honey and feta

Nutritional values: kcal: 256 Carbohydrates: 3 g Protein: 9 g Fat: 23 g

Ingredients:

- 4 lettuce hearts
- 2 stalks of parsley
- 200 g feta cheese
- 200 g cherry tomatoes
- 3 tbsp lemon juice
- 3 tbsp olive oil
- 2 tbsp pine nuts
- 2 tbsp sour cream
- 1 tbsp liquid honey
- salt
- pepper
- sugar

Preparation:

1. Toast the pine nuts in a pan without fat until golden brown and take them out.

2. Crumble the feta and stir it with sour cream and honey.

3. Cut the tomatoes in half.

4. Halve the lettuce hearts.

5. Chop the parsley.

6. Mix them with lemon juice, 1 tablespoon of water, salt, pepper and 1 teaspoon of sugar. Beat in oil.

7. Arrange the lettuce hearts on plates.

8. Spread the feta cream and tomatoes on top.

9. Put the seeds on top and drizzle the lemon marinade over them.

After-work salad with ground beef

Nutritional values: kcal: 340 Carbohydrates: 12 g Protein: 27 g Fat: 20 g

Ingredients:

- 1 red pointed pepper
- 1 red onion
- 1 mini romaine lettuce
- 1 can of corn, bell pepper and kidney bean mix
- 350 g ground beef
- 250 g whole milk yogurt
- 3 tbsp lime juice
- 1 tbsp oil
- salt
- pepper
- Cayenne pepper
- sugar

Preparation:

1. Fry the mince in oil until it is crumbly.
2. Season it with salt, pepper, and cayenne pepper.
3. Drain the corn mix.
4. Cut the lettuce into strips.
5. Cut the peppers into rings.
6. Cut the onion into strips.
7. Season the yogurt with lime juice, salt, cayenne pepper, and sugar.
8. Mix the prepared ingredients with the yogurt and serve everything.

Fiery shrimp pan

Nutritional values: kcal: 189 Carbohydrates: 9 g Protein: 23 g Fat: 6 g

Ingredients:

- 3 zucchini
- 3 chili peppers
- 1 bunch of spring onions
- 1 bunch of parsley
- 5 cloves of garlic
- 400 g frozen, raw shrimp (without head and shell)
- 300 g cherry tomatoes
- 3 tbsp olive oil
- salt
- pepper

Preparation:

1. Rinse the shrimp in a colander.
2. Let them thaw on a plate.
3. Cut the zucchini into pieces.
4. Cut the spring onions into rings.
5. Halve the garlic and tomatoes.
6. Cut the chili peppers into strips.
7. Chop the parsley.
8. Heat 2 tablespoons of oil in a pan and fry the prawns vigorously for 2 to 3 minutes on all sides and transfer them to a plate.
9. Add 1 tablespoon of oil to the frying fat and fry the onions and zucchini on all sides.
10. Add the tomatoes, garlic, and chili peppers.
11. Add the shrimp back in.
12. Season everything with salt and pepper and sprinkle with parsley.

Chicken skewer on a colorful garden salad with a herb and sour cream dressing

Nutritional values: kcal: 202 Carbohydrates: 5 g Protein: 13 g Fat: 13 g

Ingredients:

- ½ small cucumber
- 1 head of kohlrabi
- 1 chicken fillet
- 6 stems mixed herbs
- ½ glass of baby corn
- 200 g baby romaine lettuce
- 100 g sour cream
- 5 tbsp milk
- 2 tablespoons oil
- salt
- pepper
- Lemon juice
- sugar
- Paprika powder

Preparation:

1. Cut the cucumber and kohlrabi into thin slices.
2. Cut the lettuce into small pieces.
3. Chop the herbs.
4. Mix everything with the milk and sour cream.
5. Season to taste with salt and pepper as well as the lemon juice and sugar.
6. Cut the fillets into strips.
7. Put the fillets on wooden skewers and season them with salt, pepper and a little paprika.
8. Heat oil in a pan and fry the skewers on all sides for 3 to 4 minutes.
9. Drain the corn on the cob.
10. Mix them with the cucumber mixture and the salad.
11. Arrange the chicken skewers on the salad and sprinkle them with the dressing.

Salmon steak in a bed of leeks

Nutritional values: kcal: 356 Carbohydrates: 5 g Protein: 29 g Fat: 24 g

Ingredients:

- 4 pieces of salmon fillet
- 1 yellow pepper
- 1 onion
- 2 leeks without "green"
- 100 g sour cream
- 2 tablespoons oil
- salt
- pepper
- sugar
- Paprika powder

Preparation:

1. Cut the pepper and onion into cubes.
2. Cut the leek into rings.
3. Season the fish with salt and pepper.
4. Heat 1 tablespoon of oil in a pan.
5. Add the bell pepper and onion and sauté both for 2 minutes.
6. Add the leek.
7. Stir in the cream.
8. Season everything with salt, pepper and sugar.

9. Let it simmer for 4 minutes.
10. Heat 1 tablespoon of oil in another pan and fry the fish on all sides for 5 minutes over medium heat.
11. Season the vegetables with paprika powder.
12. Arrange the s on a plate and add the fish.

Quick zucchini salad

Nutritional values: kcal: 307 Carbohydrates: 5 g Protein: 25 g Fat: 22 g

Ingredients:

- 4 smoked mackerel fillets
- 1 clove of garlic
- 1 chilli pepper
- 800 g yellow and green zucchini
- 4 tbsp balsamic vinegar
- 2 tbsp olive oil
- 1 tsp sugar
- salt
- pepper

Preparation:

1. Chop the garlic.
2. Chop the chili pepper.
3. Mix the vinegar with sugar, garlic, and chili.
4. Beat in some oil.
5. Season the whole thing with salt and pepper.
6. Slice the zucchini into thin strips.
7. Mix the zucchini with the vinaigrette.
8. Arrange them on a plate.
9. Divide the mackerel fillets into pieces.

Whole grain bread with cottage cheese and avocado

Nutritional values: kcal: 490 Carbohydrates: 1 g Protein: 9 g Fat: 1 g

Ingredients:

- 2 slices of wholemeal bread
- 60 g of cottage cheese
- 1 stick of thyme
- ½ avocado
- ½ lime
- Chili flakes
- salt
- pepper

Preparation:

1. Cut the avocado in half.
2. Remove the pulp and cut it into slices.
3. Pour the lime juice over it.

4. Wash the thyme and shake it dry.

5. Remove the leaves from the stem.

6. Brush the whole wheat bread with the cottage cheese.

7. Place the avocado slices on top.

8. Top with the chili flakes and thyme.

9. Season everything with salt and pepper and serve.

Porridge with walnuts

Nutritional values: kcal: 378 Carbohydrates: 1 g Protein: 8 g Fat: 7 g

Ingredients:

- 50 g raspberries
- 50 g blueberries
- 25 g of ground walnuts
- 20 g of crushed flaxseed
- 10 g of oatmeal
- 200 ml nut drink
- Agave syrup
- ½ teaspoon cinnamon
- salt

Preparation:

1. Warm the nut drink in a small saucepan.

2. Add the walnuts, flaxseed, and oatmeal, stirring constantly.

3. Stir in the cinnamon and salt.

4. Let everything simmer for 5 to 8 minutes.

5. Keep stirring everything.

6. Sweet the whole thing.

7. Put the porridge in a bowl.

8. Wash the berries and let them drain.

9. Add them to the porridge and serve everything.

Bread with zucchini

Nutritional values: kcal: 130 Carbohydrates: 1 g Protein: 9 g Fat: 1 g

Ingredients:

- 3 eggs
- 1 zucchini
- 1 banana
- 150 g ground almonds
- 1 tbsp raisins
- 3 teaspoons of honey
- 1 ½ tsp baking powder
- 1 teaspoon coconut oil
- 1 teaspoon cinnamon
- salt

Preparation:

1. Clean and grate the zucchini.

2. Add some salt and let the whole thing steep.

3. Then squeeze the zucchini well.

4. Put the eggs, banana, honey, and coconut oil in a large bowl.

5. Mix it all up.

6. Add the raisins and zucchini.

7. Mix everything.

8. Put the ground almonds, baking powder, salt, and cinnamon in another bowl and stir everything together.

9. Add the almond mixture to the egg mixture.

10. Mix everything into a batter.

11. Grease a loaf pan with the coconut oil.

12. Put in the batter.

13. Preheat the oven to 180 degrees.

14. Bake the bread for 35 to 40 minutes.

15. Let it cool, release it from the mold, and serve.

Low carb loaf bread with pumpkin seeds

Nutritional values: kcal: 260 Carbohydrates: 1 g Protein: 1 g Fat: 7 g

Ingredients:

- 5 eggs
- 250 g low-fat quark
- 200 g ground almonds
- 150 g of crushed flax seeds
- 25 g of ground pumpkin seeds
- 2 tbsp pumpkin seeds
- 2 tbsp sunflower seeds
- 1 packet of baking powder
- 2 teaspoons of salt
- 1 teaspoon cocoa powder
- ½ teaspoon cumin

Preparation:

1. Put all the dry ingredients in a bowl and mix them together.

2. Put the curd and eggs in a second bowl and whisk them together.

3. Add the dry ingredients and work everything into a dough.

4. Line a loaf pan with parchment paper.

5. Fill in the batter.

6. Spread the remaining pumpkin seeds over it and press them down lightly.

7. Preheat the oven to 160 degrees.

8. Bake the bread for 50 to 60 minutes.

9. Take the bread out of the mold and let it cool.

Aztec rolls with quark dip

Nutritional values: kcal: 190 Carbohydrates: 4 g Protein: 9 g Fat: 8 g

Ingredients:

- 500 g quark
- 2 eggs
- 6 tbsp chia seeds
- 6 tbsp flaxseed
- salt
- pepper
- 3 spring onions
- 1 bunch of chives
- 1 bunch of parsley
- 150 g crème fraîche
- 3 teaspoons of pumpkin seeds
- 2 tsp sunflower seeds

Preparation:

1. Put half of the quark, eggs, chia seeds, flax seeds, ½ teaspoon salt and ½ teaspoon pepper in a bowl.
2. Mix well and let it soak for 20 minutes.
3. Clean the onions and cut them into fine rings.
4. Wash the chives and cut them into fine rolls.
5. Wash and chop the parsley.
6. For the dip, place the other half of the quark, the crème fraîche, and half of the chives and parsley in another bowl.
7. Mix together the ingredients for the dip and season with salt and pepper.
8. For the rolls, roughly chop the pumpkin seeds and mix them with the sunflower seeds.
9. Add the onions and the rest of the herbs and stir in.
10. Line a baking sheet with parchment paper and put 10 piles of the mixture on top.
11. Flatten them and sprinkle the seeds over them.
12. Preheat the oven to 180 degrees.
13. Bake the buns for 25 minutes and then let them cool.
14. Serve the whole thing with the dip.

Porridge with coconut flour

Ingredients:

- 1 egg
- ½ vanilla pod
- 75 g coconut flour
- 25 g desiccated coconut
- 400 ml of water
- 50 ml of cream
- Agave syrup

Preparation:

1. Put the coconut flour, desiccated coconut, and the pulp of the vanilla pod in a saucepan.
2. Stir in the cream and water.
3. Heat the whole thing and let it cook for 3 minutes over medium heat, stirring constantly.
4. Beat the egg and stir it in with a whisk.
5. Heat the whole thing again for a moment.
6. Season everything with the agave syrup and top it with a topping of your choice.

Porridge with almonds and flax seeds

Ingredients:

- 60 g ground almonds
- 200 ml coconut milk
- 200 ml of water
- 4 tbsp crushed flaxseed
- 1 tbsp chia seeds
- salt
- Agave syrup

Preparation:

1. Heat the coconut milk and water in a saucepan.
2. Add the flax seeds, ground almonds, and chia seeds.
3. Season the whole thing with a little salt.
4. Let the whole boil for 8 minutes, stirring constantly.
5. Sweeten it with the agave syrup and serve.

Omelette with goat cheese and walnuts

Nutritional values: kcal: 524 Carbohydrates: 7 g Protein: 27 g Fat: 40 g

Ingredients:

- 8 eggs
- 2 red onions
- ½ bunch of spring onions
- 200 g camembert
- 50 g walnut kernels
- 5 tbsp whipped cream
- 6 teaspoons maple syrup
- 3 teaspoons of oil
- salt
- pepper

Preparation:

1. Peel the onions and cut them into rings.
2. Cut the goat cheese into 8 slices.
3. Whisk the eggs and cream together well. Season them with salt and pepper.
4. Roast the walnuts in a non-fat coated pan. Take them out.
5. Add 1 teaspoon of oil to the pan and heat it up.
6. Fry the onions in the oil and remove them.
7. Heat ½ teaspoon oil in the pan.
8. Add a quarter of the egg-cream mixture and let the whole thing covered for 5 minutes and set over low heat.
9. Take out the mixture.
10. Spread a quarter of the onion mixture and 2 slices of goat cheese on one half of the omelet.
11. Cut off the other half and keep the whole thing warm.
12. Repeat for the other 3 omelets.
13. Then arrange everything with the nuts and syrup.

Baked Eggs Avocado with Tomato Salsa

Nutritional values: kcal: 480 Carbohydrates: 9 g Protein: 14 g Fat: 44 g

Ingredients:

- 4 eggs
- 2 avocados
- 1 red onion
- 6 slices of bacon
- 200 g tomatoes
- 2 tbsp white wine vinegar
- 1 tbsp olive oil
- 2 teaspoons of lemon juice
- salt
- pepper
- sugar
- Tabasco

Preparation:

1. Preheat the oven to 175 degrees and set it to convection.
2. Line a tray with paper.
3. Halve the avocado lengthways.
4. Remove the core.
5. Brush the cut surfaces with the lemon juice.
6. Cut off a piece of peel from the bottom so that the avocado stands firmly on the baking sheet.
7. Place the avocado on the baking sheet.
8. Season the cut surfaces with salt and pepper.
9. Break open the eggs one at a time and slide one of them into one of the hollows.
10. Bake everything in the oven for 20 minutes.
11. For the salsa, peel the onions.
12. Cut the onions into cubes.
13. Wash the tomatoes and cut them into cubes.
14. Mix the onions with the tomatoes.
15. Add salt, pepper, sugar, vinegar and Tabasco.
16. Stir in the oil.
17. Cut the bacon into thin slices.
18. Fry the bacon in a pan without fat until crispy.
19. Take the avocado out of the oven and season the eggs with a little salt and pepper.
20. Pour the bacon on top and serve with the salsa.

Chia Flea Egg White Buns

Ingredients:

For the dough:

- 1 egg
- 100 g low-fat quark

- 75 g protein powder
- 30 g chia seeds
- 15 g psyllium husks
- 140 ml of water
- ½ pack of baking powder
- 1½ tsp salt

Preparation:

1. Mix the dry ingredients for the batter.
2. Mix the wet ingredients in another bowl.
3. Mix the dry and wet ingredients together and mix them into a batter.
4. Let the dough stand for 5 minutes.
5. Line a baking sheet with baking paper and preheat the oven to 180 degrees.
6. Place the ingredients on a medium-sized plate to sprinkle.
7. Shape the dough into small balls and roll them in the ingredients to sprinkle.
8. Then place the balls on the tray and flatten them a little.
9. Bake the buns at 180 degrees for 15 to 20 minutes.

www.ingramcontent.com/pod-product-compliance
Lightning Source LLC
Chambersburg PA
CBHW080912160726
48000CB00009B/2961